Exercises in the 22nd Edition of the DEWEY DECIMAL CLASSIFICATION

M P Satija
Guru Nanak Dev University

Ess Ess Publications

4837/24, Ansari Road, Darya Ganj,
New Delhi-110002
✆ : 23260807
Fax : 23274173
E-mail: info@essessreference.com
url:http://www.essessreference.com

First Published 2004

ISBN: 81-7000-419-5

Rs.400/-

Published by:
Ess Ess Publications
4837/24, Ansari Road, Darya Ganj,
New Delhi-110 002.
Phone: 23260807
Fax: 23274173
E-mail: info@essessreference.com
url: http://www.essessreference.com

Printed in India at:
Printline, New Delhi

Contents

Dedicated
with profound regards
to

Päivi Pekkarinen

Preface

"It's a big world. We've organised it".

– OCLC

A system of library classification whose technique flashed across the inquiring mind of young Melvil Dewey (1851-1931) on a fine May morning in 1873 is still the most popular one the world over. Soon after its publication in 1876, its popularity spread across the globe. At present, it is estimated to be used in 2 lakh libraries and information centres in about 135 countries in every corner of the world. Sixty two national bibliographies are arranged by the DDC. The sun never sets on the DDC empire! Now it is trying to find many uses outside the library, e.g., organising information on the Internet. Even a hotel is now organised on Dewey's Decimal System*.

Historically speaking, modern library classification begins with the DDC. It provides a paradigm to all the library classification systems that have come up in its wake. Classification by discipline (also depicting hierarchic relations), ingenious use of decimal notation, and the relative index are its enduring contributions which have been borrowed by all the later classifications as their very basis. Some have improved upon it in some ways but faltered in others. None could catch up with its popularity, however. Despite criticism of its 19th century structure, its popularity has always shown an ascending graph. Popularity is based upon simplicity and efficacy. Not only this, the invention of the DDC has played a vital role in giving direction and shape to modern librarianship. It is not for nothing that Melvil Dewey is given the title: Father of modern librarianship!

---

* The Library Hotel, New York www.libraryhotel.com

Revision of the DDC is institutionalised, and so is a continuous process. It has undergone constant revisions to keep itself abreast of the ever advancing frontiers of knowledge and to cater to the increasing demand of its users. The 23rd edition is presently under way. In every revision, it has been expanded, modified, rectified, and made more modern in its methods and outlook and format. Since Dewey, it has come a long way in its endeavours to meet the needs of society overwhelmed by the information revolution. It has been translated into about 35 languages including almost all the major languages of the world, ranging from Vietnamese, Hebrew, Arabic, Hindi and Thai to French, German, Italian, Spanish and Russian. In many countries, its relevant portions have been recast and expanded to suit their local needs. Some of such adaptations and home-made expansions are officially recognised. The system is taught in library schools all over the world.

Yet many librarians criticise it for its enumerative pattern. The criticism is now only partially valid. They plead to abandon it or not to adopt it but fail to provide a better alternative. Frustrated, they declare classification as an impossibility or absurdity. Many a critical storm has raged to uproot it. Always it has come out unscathed. At times, it was forsaken by some to be readopted later. Deserters had to comeback to its fold, eventually. Once declared dead, it is now pulsating with a vigorous life. It is living and kicking and is a very influencing system in many ways. The system has been modernised and geared up to play its role in the Information Society of the 21st century.

Notwithstanding the fashion to criticise it, the system has become the very marrow in the bones that a librarian make. It has become an institution of librarianship as it now involves many shades of the community of librarians in its making. It is the only gateway to learn the theory and practice of library classification; and for many it is the end. For many others, the DDC means the classification.

One of the repeated charge is that having no philosophy of its own, it is not based on any theory. This is partially true. Nevertheless, the DDC is a practical scheme that answers the basic problems of classifying and arranging information in libraries.

The DDC has over the years given rise to many interesting and revealing theoretical studies. A good part of total classification literature is exclusively devoted to this system. It invariably constitutes a central chapter in any book on general classification. Examples are cited from its schedules to show classification methods. Some of its studies have shed light on the socio-politico-cultural bearings of classification. It has been a subject of some doctoral dissertations, many research projects and exclusive conferences and workshops. The tide of literature on the DDC is constantly swelling. Attention is drawn to Sushma Gupta's bibliography of more than 700 items exclusive on the DDC: *Decimal Classification System: A Bibliography for the Period 1876-1994*. March 1995. URL: http://www.oclc.org/dewey*.

In the 22nd edition released in September 2003, the DDC has been further modernised both conceptually and physically. It has been simultaneously made available in traditional print edition (of 4 volumes) and electronic edition through the Internet called *WebDewey*. It is a hi tech but user friendly edition which has more and clear notes, more interdisciplinary numbers, improved and enhanced relative index and an expanded Manual. The manual entries are also included in the relative index. Vocabulary reflects international usage. Internationalisation and users' convenience are its hallmarks.

The present book aims to introduce the students to the process of assigning and especially synthesising class numbers by the 22nd edition of the DDC. The chapters and the examples have been graded to some extent. No background, whatsoever,

---

* Sushma Gupta: *Decimal Classification System: a bibliography for the period 1876-1994*. New Delhi: M.D. Publications, 1997, pp. 122.

has been assumed on the part of the reader. Though it aims at the beginner, yet it provides a complete course to train the students in the techniques of number building involving the use of various auxiliary tables and multiple synthesis. A chapter each has been devoted to the structure of the DDC and subject analysis of the documents to be classified. Alternative class numbers have also been given whenever official options allow. The graded process of number building may mirror before the students the increasing faceted nature of the system and its advancing steps towards what S.R. Ranganathan terms as depth classification. To avoid long discussions the number building has been depicted through equations and facet formulas. This may mentally stimulate the students. It is hoped that in this way the student will learn the ropes of the DDC through this how-to-do-it text.

In this edition new examples have been added from revised classes of 004-006 Data processing (in computer science), 200 Religion, 305-306 Social groups and institutions, 340 Law, 510 Mathematics especially 518 Numerical analysis, and 610 Medicine. The chapter on the Relative Index has been simplified. The examples, chosen of necessity, are largely imaginary, though not far from the realities of literary warrant. The aim is to be amply illustrative and to introduce step-by-step all the concepts and methods of the DDC. In the process some repetition was inevitable, for which the forbearance of the readers is sought. Another aim is to be simple and clear. It is admitted that to write simply has been as simple and difficult as writing on "how to lace a shoe".

The book is based on the 22nd edition of the DDC. But it is expected that an intelligent student is able to adapt this book to other recent editions.

Suggestions for improvement are earnestly requested.

M P S

satija_mp@yahoo.com

Acknowledgement

Grateful thanks are to all the students and teachers of classification in India who have constantly given encouraging feedback to keep the work updated and in print.

Mr. Peter J. Paulson (retired, Director Forest Press, Dr. Frau Inge Dahlberg have always been a source of inspiration on classification studies. It is long time Dr. John Comaromi (1937-1991) left for his heavenly abode, he is sadly missed whenever I work on this book. Ms Paivi Pekkarinen gets a full page.

Prof. MTM Khan (of Bundhel Khand University), Prof. C.P. Vashisth (Delhi Library Association) Prof. Shabahat Husain (Aligarh Muslim University), Prof. M. Parameswaran (Calicut University), Prof. I.V. Malhan (Jammu University), Dr. Jagtar Singh (Punjabi University) and Dr. N.S. Shokeen (of Haryana Polytechnic) all eminent teachers of classification, have generously lent time and expertise on some contentious issues. They have helped to improve the work, though its shortcomings and omissions, if any, are mine.

Salient Features of the DDC 22 (2003)

With 127 + years of eventful and checkered history past it, the DDC is the oldest living yet thriving modern library classification. It has undergone 21+ revisions, and is the most applied one. Apart from its use in two lac libraries in more than 135 countries across the six continents, many national and trade bibliographies use it for organising their contents. Now it has made successful forays into the world of electronic documents and networked information.

The 22nd edition was released in September 2003, two months later than the announced time of July 2003. However, its electronic version WebDewey was released on time in July. The period between two print editions now seems settled to a seven years as a matter of policy. CD versions of the Dewey were issued annually whereas WebDewey i.e. Dewey accessible only via the internet is updated quarterly.

So what constitutes an edition is now legally a problematic question. Edition is rolling, always in a flux without much fixity.

Since the last half a century especially during the tenure of Benjamin A Custer (1912-1997) as editor (1956-1980; Editions 16-19) it has been an era of structural changes in the DDC backed by professional management and organisational planning. Custer was instrumental in not only resuscitating but also putting DDC back on the path of progress. His able successor Dr. John Comaromi (1937-1991) who edited the 20th edition (1989) ushered in a period of simplification and consolidation. Since the acquisition of the Forest Press by the OCLC in 1988 a lot more research input goes into making a new edition of the DDC. If the DDC 21 (1996) was a product of high IT, the 22nd edition can safely be termed as child of network technology. It is the first edition produced in the web environment. Editors and policy makers got constant feedback and suggestions via the net to add new features and to achieve accuracy and efficiency. To be abreast of current developments on knowledge practices the editors relied on the Internet and electronic databases for new topics and terms.

Its electronic version WebDewey (2003) and Abridged WebDewey (2004) are now only available on the Internet to the licensed users. The annually updated *Dewey for Windows*, on CD ceased publication in 2001. This decision may hurt the libraries in developing countries where the Internet, due to poor telecommunication infrastructure and unreliable services, is not easily accessible.

It is a second edition edited in a row by Joan S. Mitchell who took over as editor in 1993. It carries forward the policies and improvement started earlier in DDC 21 especially its onslaught on the Christian and western cultural bias in the schedules and tables. Two editions plan for reducing the Christian bias in 200 religion started in DDC 21 has now been completed with some additional provisions in 296 and 297.

Organisation of the System

The print DDC 22 in four volumes containing 4076 pages in all has been divided into eleven sections marked A/K as follows :

Volume 1 Sections A/G

A	xi-xxxvi	Prefatory text, notes and new features
B	xxxvii - lxiii	Introduction to the system of the DDC

C	lxv - lxxiv	Glossary : Brief definitions of terms used in the theory and practice of the DDC
D	lxxv - lxxvii	Index to the terms and concepts in sections A/C.
E	1-181	Manual : A guide to the interpretation and comprehension of some ambiguous numbers; to compare and contrast two analogous or seemingly similar subjects in the schedules and tables.
F	183-713	Six tables with their subdivisions
G	715-731	Equivalence table of relocated and reused numbers from the previous edition

Volume 2 Section H & I

H	v-xvi	Three main Summaries
I	1-1250	Schedules of classes 000-599

Volume 3 Section J

J	1-1074	Schedules of classes 600-999

Volume 4 Section K

K	1-928	Relative index : Alphabetical and structural index of subjects and topics listed in context of disciplines and their corresponding numbers in schedules and tables

New Features

The new edition, as expected represents the current thinking in knowledge mapping and emergence of new terminology. Progress made in understanding the user approaches in accessing information and users expectations from such a tool has been the focus of this new edition. The revision process has received considerable input from a commissioned survey of the DDC users in USA, Canada, UK and Australia, conducted by George D'Elia (of the State University of New York (SUNY), at Buffalo). In addition to the D'Elia's survey the Editorial Policy Committee (DCEPC) which is both a recommendatory and supervising committee, and an apex body to approve any change continued to associate outside experts, institutions and associations for suggestions on some national and cultural issues and to reduce inherent biases. It is a healthy trend to involve *inter alia* experts from other knowledge organisation tools, e.g. Professor I.C. McIlwaine (UDC) and Dr. Joseph Miller (Sears List) in the review process. International survey has led to improvements in geographic areas, laws, political systems and parties, languages, literatures and historical periods. Wide based cooperation helps the expanding translation programme and in using current terminology. Concern for users convenience continues - though no new special or user friendly device or move has been incorporated. Only number of multilevel summaries has been increased which facilitate scanning and subsequent location of a number without undue scurry. Apart from outsourcing revision and advise, a few areas were also pretested in some US and foreign libraries.

Acquisition of the DDC by the OCLC in 1988 has meant a great deal of progress for the former. It has inaugurated an era of research, new products and services and their organised marketing. The OCLC Office of Research had involved itself in classification research at the beginning of the revision, especially in the harmonisation of various knowledge classification systems, mapping of DDC numbers to subject headings, above all to make DDC amenable to organise electronic information of every sort. In addition to the feedback and expert advice, this edition, as usual, is based on actual classification of three quarters of a million current books in the Decimal Classification Division of the Library of Congress since 1996.

Changes

The first and noticeable change is with the publisher. The Forest Press (incorporated 1932), a subsidiary of the OCLC since July 1988, has been retired and the work has been published direct by the OCLC. It seemed something on the way since the retirement of Peter J. Paulson and shifting of the Forest Press from Albany to OCLC headquarter at Dublin, Ohio. The other outstanding change has been the abrogation of the Table 7 Persons. Its contents have been shifted partially to the standard subdivision T1-08, and for the rest use of the add from 011-999 instruction is made. What good this move has done is not clear. In fact it has made number building in some cases bit circuitous especially while using Table 3C. It has also resulted in the reuse of many DDC 21 numbers with new meanings :

Title	*DDC 21*	*DDC 22*
Artworks by Scientists	704+5(T7) = 704.5	704.08+8 (from 088 T1) + 5 (001 - 999) = 704.0885
Ethics of historians	174.9+97(T7) = 174.997	174.9 + 90720 (from 907 = 201) + 2 (T2) = 174.9907202
Collection of English poetry about lawyers	821.0080352344	821.008035208834

However, some numbers remain the same e.g., Social customs of artists 390.47 (both DDC21 and DDC 22). A few numbers have also become shorter in length.

But certainly there are improvements in the manual

now shifted to volume 1 (pp 1-182) from the fourth in DDC 21. Notes in the manual have been shortened with removal of some redundant information, and further by dividing them into smaller sections. Some information from the manual has been transferred as notes to the respective entries in the schedules and tables. This has helped prune redundant information. The manual now makes more clear and easy reading. Flow charts, builtin numbers, and *see also*, references are of great help to classifiers in achieving inter-indexer consistency.

The relative index of 928 pages has 33 pages more than the previous index to include new builtin numbers and some additional terms. Entry vocabulary is wide based and current. The index has been beefed up.

In compliance with the recommendations of D Elia's survey all the works relating to directories of travel facilities such as hotels, lodges, motels, inns, have been shifted to 910.46 and to 913/919, whereas 647.94 continues to be in place for hotels, etc, *per se*.

Unlike the previous editions (trend that started in DDC 16) there are no full class or extensive revisions (nee' phoenix schedules) in the DDC 22. But minor changes are many. Some routine revisions involving expansions, reduction, deletions and relocations are outlined here :

004-006 Data processing and computer science. New topics have been accommodated retaining the structure.

200 Two editions programme of removing Christian bias and further expansion of 296 and 297 is now complete. Contents of 291 Comparative religion have now been distributed to 200-209 with obviously brief numbers, and more space for expansions. As a result standard subdivisions of 200 have been shifted to 200.1-.9.

340	Law. Now 341 international law becomes law of nations with new numbers for human rights and inter governmental organisations.
510	Mathematics (earlier completely revised in DDC 18(1971)) has been substantially updated. Numerical analysis earlier part of 515 has been upgraded and shifted to 518 lying vacant since long.
543	All aspects of Analytical chemistry dispersed earlier have been converged at 543.1-543.8
610	It has been reworded as "Medicine and health", and medical topics find improved indexing.
640	It is now titled as "Home and family management" with some topics shifted to 910 travels.
930-990	The historical periods have been updated
T2	The Area table has been updated by geographic areas, historical periods and persons
T5 and T6	From T5 by deleting the term "Racial" the table has been renamed as "National and ethnic groups". These tables have been expanded especially to make provisions for American native people and languages.

However, these changes are not those projected as slated changes for DDC 22 in the DDC 21 (1996), namely in 520 Astronomy, 355-359 Military science, 636-639 Animal husbandry and 690 Buildings. Obviously switch over to the DDC 22 will put less strain on libraries.

Abridged edition 14 released in early 2004 is a true abridgement of the DDC meant to classify a general collection upto 20,000 documents. Its web version abridged WebDewey (www.oclc.org/info/abridged14) has been issued simultaneously. WebDewey is an enhanced version of the Dewey database of terms and numbers available in the print edition. Updated quarterly, it is only accessible via the Internet on annual subscription basis. It provides much more facilities including keyword navigation. Annotation feature allows classifiers to add and share notes about local classification changes. WebDewey is available within the full OCLC cataloguing services environment. It provides many access points with many search and browse indexes. It makes the location of Dewey numbers an easy game.

DDC 22, the first edition of this millennium, has kept pace with the fast changing information environment to map and organise it squarely.

References

1. *Dewey Decimal Classification and Relative Index* - 22nd ed/ed. by Joan S. Mitchell, *et. al.* Dublin, OH. : OCLC, 2003. 4v (lxxvii, 731 p; xvi, 1250 p.; 1074 p ; 934 p) ISBN 0-910608-70-9 (Hb).
2. www.oclc.org/dewey
3. www.oclcl.org/info/abridged14/
4. Comaromi, John P, *et. al. A survey of the use of the Dewey Decimal Classification in the United States and Canada.* Lake Placid, N.Y.: Forest Press, 1975, x, 290p (mimeogrephed).
5. Lawson, Dawn. "Abridged WebDewey brings electronic classification to smaller libraries" *OCLC Newsletter* March/April 2002 : 13.
6. Mitchell, Joan S. "DDC 22 offers many updates to Dewey Users Worldwide" *OCLC News letter* July 2003 : 16-19.

Bibliography

1. Shokeen, Ashu and Kaushik, Sanjay K. "DDC 22: how it differs from the DDC 21" *Lib. Herald* 42(1) March 2004 : 67-74.
2. Srivastava, Rochna. "Enhanced DDC 22 and WebDewey : the power of Dewey on the Web" *Herald of Lib Sc* 43 (1/2) 2004 : 12 - 17.

1

Introduction to the Text of Four Volumes

Since the 20th edition (1989) the print versions of the DDC (full edition) have continued to be in four volumes.* The four volumes of the DDC 22 forming a total of 4076 pages (DDC 21 had 4126) (including prefatory material) have been organised into four volumes as follows :

Volume 1. The first volume of lxxvii + 731 pages contains the prefatory material by the Chairman DCEPC (xi-xviii pages), the "New Features in the Edition 22" (xix - xxxvi pages). Introduction (pp, xxxvii-lxii) to the DDC is a sort of operational manual including its theory and philosophy which has been

---

* The first edition (1876) of the DDC was a thin pamphlet of 44 pages; and the second edition (1885) was seven times as large as that. Growth continued and the unwieldy size of the 14th edition (1942) became a source of worry for many. The 15th edition (1951) was an exercise to trim the system to a standard edition, which proved a *faux pas* by every account. To cope with the alarmingly increasing size, the sixteenth edition (1958) was issued in two volumes - the second volume contained the form divisions, area table, and the index. The eighteenth edition (1971) was issued, for the first time, in three volumes, so was the nineteenth (1970).

further simplied in this edition. Glossary of terms and concepts (pp, lxv - lxxiv) used in the preceeding chapters is brief explanation of terms in theory and preface of the DDC. Rest of the pages are devoted to the manual (pp 1 - 714) and a ready recknor of relocated and discontinued numbers between DDC-21 and 22 (pp 715 - 731).

Volumes 2 - 3. These two volumes are devoted to the schedules of classes. The volume 2 of pages xvi + 1250 lists classes 001 - 599. The schedules are prefaced by three major summaries, namely, Ten main classes (First Summary), Hundred Divisions (Second Summary), and Thousand Sections (Third summary). These summaries help to visualise at a glance the mapping and structure of universe of knowledge or its portions as depicted in the DDC. In fact the summaries both in theory and practice have been so useful that the editors have carried summaries to lower levels (multi level summaries) in the schedules and tables. The third volume contains schedules of classes 600 - 999. The schedules are arranged in 001 to 999 order, and the section number is always printed at top of every page, as it is more convenient to scan the schedules by class numbers. Schedules have been defined as "The series of numbers constituting the notation for the ten main DDC classes and all their subdivisions". This is in fact a full burgeoning of the Ten Main classes in hierarchical order. This may be called the *terra firma* of the system, for to learn the practice of the DDC is to learn to operate it. Each entry contains a class number on the left, and on its right is given the caption, i.e. the content of the number. The subordination and coordination relations among the subjects are shown by the length of the class number on the left and the shifting of indention of the captions to the right. Under many of the class numbers there are a variety of notes of "explanations and instructions". To assign and build a correct class number these notes are essential.

Volume 4. Its 928 pages contain the Relative Index

(DDC 21's had 895 pages). The Relative Index is considered to be one of the enduring contributions of Melvil Dewey. It is a great help to classifiers, and many prefer to approach the Schedules through the Index. The Index is called relative as it brings together all aspects of a single topic which have otherwise been scattered by discipline in the Schedules. Hence, the Schedules and the Index are complementary to one another.

TYPES OF ENTRIES

All the approximate 30000 entries in the schedules may be divided into six categories.

1. Ordinary entries (used headings)
2. Unusable headings (not to be used)
3. Unassigned numbers : Number without a classes
4. Optional entries : Providing alternative numbers
5. Hooked numbers
6. Centered heading

1. Ordinary entries

Most of the entries in the system are ordinary entries : a number with a corresponding heading which may or may not have notes or instructions. These are applied numbers.

2. Unusable headings

Consequence of revision a part of a class may be relocated to some other place or discontinued. Such a part number is enclosed within a square bracket. (See notes 13 and 14 in this chapter i.e. discontinued and relocation notes).

3. Unassigned number

A division or a section in whole may be vacant of any meaning. These, termed as unassigned numbers are enclosed in a square bracket along with a note indicating the edition when it was last used or assigned meaning. For example :

[484] [Unassigned]
Most recently used in Edition 16

It means that section 484 has remained vacant since the 17th edition. A complete list of unassigned Division and Sections in the DDC 22 is given below :

040

Sections

007-009
013
024
029
040-049
104
112
125
132
134
136
151
157
159
163
164
216-219
237
244-245
256-258
288
291
308-309
311-312
329
376 - 377
396 - 397
416
424
426
434
444
454
464
474
484
504
517
524
544-545
574
589
604
619
626
654-656
689
699
744
756
762
768
777
804
991-992

4. Optional numbers

Some numbers in the schedules are optional giving a choice to libraries to use that or alternative number given in such a type of entry.

Wherever another place for a subject is available, this is indicated with a note "Option : Class with ...". This is an option which is not used by the Decimal Classification Division, the official laboratory of the scheme. But if it suits any individual library this option may be availed of. For example, under 016 Subject bibliographies and catalogs, one reads "Option : Class with the specific discipline or subject, using notation 016 from Table 1, e.g., bibliographies of medicine 610.16". Some critics feel that in such options the value of system as a tool of standardization is eroded. Optional numbers are enclosed within parenthesis, i.e., round bracket.

For instance, at (848.99) (vol. 3; p. 791) French language literatures not requiring local emphasis, one finds a note that the use of this number is optional for libraries. Under such notes the official preference (i.e., the class number used by the Decimal Classification Division of the LC) is also given. For example, after the instruction under (848.99), the official preference i.e. "Prefer 840-848 for all French language literatures," has also been indicated.

5. Centered headings

Sometimes a subject instead of being assigned a single class number is spread over a span of numbers, the two terminal numbers being connected by a hyphen. These centered headings or entries may occur at the section level or at its subdivisions. These are always given in the centre of the page, and on the left margin a > dingbat indicates a centered heading.

For example :

> 383-388 Communications and transportation

> 384.1-384.6 Telecommunication

It is clearly a breakdown of hierarchy but permits larger space for expanding the number. A single class number is always indicated for comprehensive works on the topic. Under 384.1-384.6, one reads the instruction "Class comprehensive works in 384". Hence the proper class number for telecommunication is 384. The device of centered headings is useful for the hospitality and brevity of notation.*

Hook number entries

Some numbers in the hierarchy of sub-divisions have no specific meaning - a concise heading which could mean a subject. Instead it could be a sort of a peg on which many other classes could be hooked or hanged by following an instruction given there. These numbers have headings such as "miscellaneous.., " "Others... ", or "specific...." In Ranganathan's Colon Classification such numbers are called quasi isolates. In chain indexing such links give out unsought headings. For example :

265.9 Other acts [Christian rites]

265.92 Consecration and dedications

265.94 Exorcism

The first is a hook number, and has only vague meaning. The other two specific numbers are hooked on it. However, this type of entry is of no practical consequences for the classifiers.

---

* Comaromi, John P. and Satija, M.P. : *Brevity of Notation in Dewey Decimal Classification*. New Delhi : Metropolitan, 1983, pp. 39-40.

* Under some of the centered headings are given a table of special subdivisions applicable to all the subdivisions appended to 785.2-785.9 specific kinds of ensembles (p. 691, vol 3).

Notes

The schedules and tables comprise of entries. Each entry apart from number/notation and its corresponding verbal heading in natural language (showing hierarchy by indentions) contains many types of notes to guide a classifier. These various types of notes help the classifier in intended interpretation of the heading regarding what it should contain and what not. The ultimate aim is to achieve uniformity and consistency in applying the DDC system. There are in all 17 kinds of notes divided into four categories :

A. Scope and Contents Notes : These includes definition, and what should be classed under that entry.

1. **Definition notes :** Such a note gives a brief but clear definition of the class. Only a few entries contain such note, e.g., see at 139 Phrenology.

2. **Scope notes :** Such notes enumerate the boundaries of the class, e.g., 516.34 Analytic trigonometry. The purpose of both these kinds of notes is the same, i.e., to bring to surface the estimate subtopics of a subject and to demarcate the boundaries of that class.

3. **Number built notes :** Some number are found synthesised in the schedule, which otherwise the classifier could have done by following instructions. In such cases the source of the synthesised number is given.

   In addition there are also some more ready made numbers in the schedules especially the ten main classes synthesised with standard subdivisions. e.g., 603 Dictionaries, etc. of Technology.

4. **Former-heading notes :** In some cases, the number, its contents and meanings remain the same but its verbal heading is changed to be in tune with current terminology. In such cases the previous heading in given with the note. "Former leading : ...".

5. **Variant-name note :** Synonymous terms are given in such notes, and these terms are also included in the relative index, e.g. 146.4 Positivism.

6. **Class-here notes :** Under a class number, sometimes there are enumerated topic(s) with the instruction "Class here...". Such topics in fact being generally broader than the class number (or overlaps other numbers), and only for convenience are to be placed there. For example, under 343.08 Regulation of trade (Commerce), besides inclusion note one reads the instruction : "Class here commodity exchanges and exchange transactions". The tenor of such notes is clear. The topics in class-here may have standard subdivisions added to them.

   It also includes the note to class interdisciplinary and comprehensive works there.

B. Inclusion notes : These types of notes indicate some additional subtopics which are to be classed under that heading.

7. **Including notes :** Some subtopics are a part of a given number may be temporarily. These are placed with the broader number because they do not possess their own number. They are given a standing room. For example, 513.211 Addition, contains the note : "Including counting...". It means that counting is not essentially a part of Addition, and yet it does not have a separate number of its own. Hence such a subject has been given a standing room till it gets its own number. No standard subdivision is to be added to such class numbers.

   Some entries may have two including-notes especially in case of Taxonomy 570-590.

C. Cross Reference Notes

These notes refer in part or whole to some other number.

8. **Class-elsewhere notes :** These are in direct contrast to

class-here notes. When a topic seemingly forming a part of a class belongs elsewhere, a note is given in the form : "Class ... in ...". For example, 181.12 Philosophy of Japan contains a note "Class Shinto philosophy in 181.09561". This also includes related note "Class comprehensive works in .... " and "class interdisciplinary works in ...."

9. **See reference :** When a seemingly part of a class is given an independent number then the classifiers are directed to that number. It begins with "For .... see", e.g. in 191 Philosophy of US and Canada, we find a note "*For middle American and Mexican philosophy.. see 199-72*" [Italics original].

10. **See also reference notes :** Obviously it refers to a related independent number for a comprehensive search, e.g.

676.285 5	Vulcanized and parchment papers
	see also 685 for parchment prepared from the skin of an animal.

[original Italics]

Such references are given on reciprocal basis, as similar note under 685 refers to 676.2845.

In a classified catalogue *See also* reference may be prepared under both the class numbers.

A *See also* note may also refer to more than one class, e.g., see under 153 Conscious mental processes and intelligence.

11. **See manual notes :** Entries in the schedules and tables are frequently linked with the manual in volume 1 of the DDC 22. This is not any cross reference but a sort of scope note for the guidance of the classifier referring to similar or analogous subjects. In the DDC 22 most of the *See manual* reference have been converted to *See also* references in the schedules, thus size of the manual

is reduced for simplicities. For example, at 305.9 occupational and miscellaneous [social] groups, we find a reference "*See Manual at 305.9 vs 305.5*"

(See also : Scope notes, and *See also* reference note)

D. Notes that explain change or irregularities

Such notes are of historical nature especially to help classifiers who switch to new edition from the previous one. These are :

12. **Revision notes :** If in a new edition a class is partially or completely revised, so a revision note is given under that class. In the DDC 22 there is no such note.

13. **Discontinued note :** Apart from some numbers given in square brackets which have no subject meaning, numbers recently discontinued are given in square brackets. Such discontinued numbers are invariably accompanied by a class-elsewhere note indicating the new number for that subject. For example, 343 [09942] Telegraph law Number discontributed class in 343.0994. It clearly means that this specific number has been merged with its broader class 343.0994 telecommunication. Its purpose is to mark changes between two successive editions to help classifiers to switch from old to the new edition.

14. **Relocation notes :** When in a new edition, as a result of relocation a subject, partially or wholly, gets a different number, its previous number is also given at the new place. The former class number is enclosed within square brackets with a prefix "*Formerly*". For example 518 Numerical Analysis [*formerly 515*] (Italics original). But when a number is partially relocated then the newly independent number is also given indicating its previous place with a note [*formerly also...*], e.g., 343.0994 telecommunication law [formerly also 341.7577]. It is

a brief history of the classification of this topic in the DDC related to this revision. It is given in the beginning of a drastically revised (phoenix) class and explains the extent of revision in the newly revised schedule.

15. **Do-not-use notes :** This kind of instruction is used when a regular place of a standard subdivision is shifted wholly or partially to some other number. If a number is wholly shifted then such a number is enclosed in square brackets. Such entries begin with a caveat "Do not use; class in ..." e.g.,

    362.[09] Historical, geographic, persons treatment. Do not use; class in 362.9

    If it applies to a partial number then the number is not enclosed in square brackets. e.g., 069.028 maintenance and repair of museum.

    Do not use maintenance and repair of museum objects; class in 069.53

16. **See-Manual notes :** Manual now shifted to volume 1 (pp 1-181) has become vital part of the DDC system and its use in correct and officially intended meaning of classes and notes in the schedules and tables cannot be gainsaid. But it is only to referred occasionally than to be read as a whole. Therefore, in the schedules and tables the classifiers are frequently referred to the relevant sections of the manual where is arranged in T1/T6; 011-999 order. This note appears in the form See manual at ...". There are numerous of them.

17. **Standard Subdivisions are added ... Notes**

A new type of note clarifying explicitly the addition of a standard subdivision to a class number was introduced in the DDC-21. It usually appears under a class number with a compound headings and explains to which part the standard subdivision, if needed, is to be added. For example :

636.37 Working and herding dogs.

Standard subdivisions are added for working and herding dogs together, for working dogs alone.

It is implied from this note that standard subdivision cannot be added to 636.37. Herding dogs. Probably herding dogs will get individual number in some future edition.

NUMBER BUILDING NOTES OR INSTRUCTIONS

This sort of note is central to the grammar of the DDC and the backbone of the synthetic apparatus in the system. Almost every class number in the DDC can be further extended whether there are immediate instructions or not. For example, the Standard Subdivisions of Table 1 may be added to any class number. In addition to such intrinsic provisions to many class numbers are provided "Add..." notes which may further be subdivided into two kinds:

1. Instructions specific to a number

Under many a class number are provided instructions for extending a basic number with some other numbers or part thereof of a class number existing elsewhere in the schedules or tables. For example, under 547.35 "Quantitative chemistry" is given the instructions" Add to base number 547.35 the numbers following 545 in 545.01-545.89". Such instructions are usually illustrated with at least one example.

2. Instructions common for a series of numbers

Sometimes a series of cognate class numbers are further extendable by another number. Instead of providing individual instructions, for convenience and simplicity, as well as for brevity of the schedules, instructions are provided at one place, while the headings of the class numbers to which such instructions apply are marked with an asterisk. Then at the foot of that page a footnote is given for the meaning of the asterisk. For example :

547.4	*Aliphatic compounds
547.41	* Hydrocarbon
547.411	* Paraffins (Alkanes)
547.412	* Olefins (Alkenes)
547.413	* Acetylenes (Alkynes)

In a footnote on the same page is given the instruction:

"* Add as instructed under 547". On going to class 547 one reads the detailed instructions : "Add to notation for each term identified by * as follows :

04	Special topics
044	Theoretical chemistry
045	Physical chemistry
046	Analytical chemistry

We can synthesis a large variety of class numbers with such provision. For example :

Theoretical chemistry of hydrocarbons

547.41 + 044 = 547.41044

Analytical chemistry of hydrocarbons

547.41 + 046 = 547.41046

Such instructions have provided a citation order of the various facets and have increased number building power.

In addition, there are instructions under many a class number to add from any of the six tables.

All these and other instructions must be carefully followed and implemented to build a correct class number.

Dot and spaces

It is generally forgotten that all the numerals used in the DDC behave like decimal fractions. The decimal point has not been put in the beginning: it is supposed to be there. But when a number gets lengthened beyond three basic digits a dot is inserted between the third and the fourth digit. This dot is only a pause and must not be misunderstood as the decimal point. It has no purpose except to break the monotony of numerals. For the same purpose, if a class number extends beyond six digits a space is left between the sixth and the seventh digit, and again between the ninth and the tenth digit, and so on. On this pattern, a space is left after every three digits coming after the dot. For example, the class number for "Supergravity" is transcribed as 530.142 3. Similarly the class number for Thyristors is transcribed as 321.381 528 7. These spaces and dot give relief to the eyes and facilitate shortwhile retention of the class number in the memory – during the passage from the catalogue to the stacks.

2

How to Assign and Build Class Numbers in the DDC

> Hold book in ryt hand and turn with left, then both class numbers and index heds show most plainly on left marjins and reference is quicker when eye follows left pages only.
>
> —*Melvil Dewey*

The work of practical classification consists of two phases: intellectual work in sorting out the specific subject of the document under classification; and the *craft* of assigning the appropriate notations to the ascertained specific subject—yes, it is a craft, an art learned over time. These two phases are respectively termed as :

(a) Subject analysis

(b) Locating class number and Number building

These two phases can be likened to medical diagnosis and prescription, respectively. If the ailment is correctly diagnosed, then prescription for its cure can safely be entrusted to skilled hands. The former is intellectual work, and for that reason the more important of the two. It is indeed the essence of classifying and somewhat independent of the classification system used. Determination of the specific subject of a given document is an art. It is no exaggeration to say that it requires intuitive insight. It only comes through a wide acquaintance with the topic and the literature upon it. Such knowledge may constantly improve through one's life, though it may never reach perfection. Indeed, widely read people have more flair than others in determining the specific subject of a book. Intense specialization and rapidly advancing frontiers of knowledge have, nevertheless, made it more difficult, if not impossible, to know everything about every subject. The specific subject of a document may be determined by examining the document under classification through its **title, sub-title, preface, blurb, table of contents, and the text itself;** the name of the author, subject index, and the cited references may also provide some valuable clues. A classifier may occasionally consult some reference tools for help in this task. If all these efforts fail, the last resort is to consult some subject expert. This so far is the work in the domain of knowledge classification. Besides determining the specific subject of a book, there may arise many difficulties to class especially a composite book at its appropriate place. For all such difficulties one can surely count on the classic book of W.S. Merrill: *Code for Classifiers: Principles Governing the Consistent Placing of Books in a System of Classification.* Chicago: A.L.A., 1939. The code is independent of any classification system.

A librarian is concerned with book classification, as distinguished from the work of knowledge classification. Therefore, for book classification, besides the knowledge of *knowledge qua knowledge,* one needs to know the structure of knowledge, its subdivisions and various adjuncts in a particular system of classification. It is the work of matchmaking: fitting in the subject into an already created place in the schedules. A classifier is essentially a match-maker. To do this is needed the schedule and the technique to consult it. Contrary to Ranganathan's views the work of a classifier is more a matter of flair than anything else. Once the specific subject is determined, there is the further need to determine the field of study in which it falls, and the way of treatment by the author in context of the classification system used: that is, determine from what view the subject has been treated. For example, a subject, say Economics, may be treated from the viewpoint of its philosophy, theory, history, research or from the practical application viewpoint. Further the above document treated from any viewpoint may be a dictionary, a journal or a mere collection of data in tabulated form. Not only this, any of the above internal or external arrangements may reach us in any of the numerous physical media, namely a book, microfiche, video cassette, a film, or a CD-ROM, now networked information. Thus a classifier has to sort out four different aspects of a given document.

(1) topic

(2) discipline

(3) point of view

(4) form*

After this is done, the only task left is to codify the subject and its treatment viewpoint into the decimal notation.

To enter the Decimal Classification the better way is through its structured ladder. The other way is through the Index. One must know at the outset (through knowledge of the scheme) to what main class, and then to what division and finally to what section of the DDC the given work pertains. For efficiency, it is better to commit to memory the 100 Divisions of the scheme. It is not absolutely necessary, though it surely lessens the avoidable leafing through the DDC Schedules to assign a class number. With experience, many of the 915 Sections (85 are empty) come on one's fingertips. In this way, we go on narrowing our approach successively at each step. Many a time we reach the section concerned

* D.W. Langridge: *Subject Analysis: Principles and Procedures*. London: Bowker-Saur, 1989.

through our personal knowledge of the scheme bypassing the scanning of the ten main classes and the divisions. If a subject is concerned with, say, education, we will go to 370 in the Schedules; and if it is concerned with medicine we look at 610 in the Schedules. Even if one is not conversant with the Divisions, this part of the class number should be worked through via the Three Summaries (given on pages v-xvi, volume 2) of the DDC. The real need to consult the Schedules arises on arriving at the correct section. To carry on the search for the appropriate and specific class number all the immediate divisions of a section, viz, subsections are further scanned, which for the convenience of the classifiers are usually given at one place. As a special feature of the DDC 22 many summaries and *multilevel summaries* have been given at the beginning of many densely detailed classes. For example, see the two-level summary of the class 570 Life sciences on pages 1057-88, Vol 2. Such summaries which are numerous are helpful to locate the desired section and subsection at one glance only. Such summaries are just like the map of a multistoried building given at the entrance. These summaries have a great reference value, and save the time and patience of the classifier in nabbing the desired class number. Multilevel summaries, a new feature since the DDC-20 are of great help in this work. These summaries also save the print schedules from physical wear and tear as the classifiers do less flipping of pages.

A classifier is like a traveller who has to select her path at every crossing where many roads diverge in various directions. By choosing the right direction at every step the classifier does not have to trudge through the whole text to reach the desired class number. In this way the minutest number available may be the specific number desired or one that may act as the base number to build further the coextensive class number matching exactly the subject of the document under classification. The further extension of the class number may be either from the auxiliary Tables or the Schedules. (This is discussed in the appropriate chapters).

To illustrate this, say our subject is "Money". At the first instance we need to examine whether the core subject of the book is Minting of money or Economics of money. If the latter is the case, a knowledgeable DDC practitioner will tell at the outset that it is a subject of social sciences, that is, of economics. On going to 330 Economics in the third summary (Volume 2, p.x) we see that it pertains to 332 Financial economics. At this stage, we shift to the schedules proper at class number 332 (Volume 2, p. 435). Examining the summary of subsections of 332 (Volume 2, p.435) we find the subsection 332.4 Money, matching squarely with the subject of the given document. Now we will shift to the subsection 332.4 (p. 441, vol 2) and scan its sub-subsections. We see here that the number 332.4 is quite appropriate. By assigning the class number 332.4 to the document our search for the appropriate and specific class number ends.

Take one more example: Anatomy of Human Lungs. The book deals with a human body organ, so in a twinkling, a practised classifier can tell that it belongs to the main class applied sciences, and then to its division medicine, which deals with the human body, its parts, and functions. Looking through the Division 610 Medicine, we find that Anatomy (which is the science of human organs) is 611, which is the desired Section. At this stage we shift our search to the Schedules at 611 (Volume 3, p.13). Looking through the summary of the subsections of 611 (on page 14 we find that 611.2 Respiratory organs is the next appropriate choice. Examining the further divisions (subsections) of 611.2 (page 17) we find Lungs enumerated at 611.24, which is our specific number.

If the subject is the Study and teaching of lungs anatomy, the Dewey classifier, will know that study and teaching is an auxiliary aspect of the core subject Lungs anatomy, and the notation for the auxiliary aspect is to be taken from Table 1: Standard subdivisions. Both notations are to be combined as per the rules.

In the Introduction the number building process has been described as a four-way technique:

1. Determine the various facets of the work
2. Determine which facets can be indicated through the notation. If all the facets cannot be included, then follow the order of precedence to select the facets for inclusion
3. Arrange the facets in the proper order. It is called Citation of facets. Citation order is always clearly explained in the number-building instructions. One has only to find the right base
4. Follow the add instructions.

If we add here the first step as determining the subject and discipline to which it belongs then it becomes the general procedure for all sorts of number building procedures.

In fact, this is too facile a view of the process of assigning a class number to a subject. In reality, a classifier may encounter many unanticipated difficulties. Firstly, it may be borne in mind that we assign class numbers not to the title but to the specific subject of the document under classification. If the title is a fanciful one and the subject has not been explained in the subtitle, the specific subject of the book must be determined from the text. For example, a book with the title "Asian Drama" could be a book of creative literature, but is a work on the economic development of the Third World. Sometimes the title may look incomplete. For example, a book may have a title "Shakespeare". At the outset one may not know whether it is the biography of William Shakespeare, or his evaluation as dramatist, or poet, or merely a collection of his works. To classify correctly one will have to supply the wanting words in the title from other parts of the text. On the other hand, there may be many superfluous words in a title. In such cases the title must be stripped of such meaningless but decorative words, and the class number be assigned only to the core words connoting the subject succinctly. For example, a book may have the title "A Long and Exciting Expedition to the Himalayas". Here Himalayan expedition is the core subject and for the purpose of classifying one will have to ignore the remaining words, however spiritually or emotionally important these may be to the author. Melvil Dewey's introduction to the 12th edition of the DDC is still valuable in this context. Ranganathan's eight steps for classifying a document may be of great help to a novice classifier.*

A difficulty in classifying may ensue from the fact that though no word in the title is redundant, yet it may not be possible to assign a co-extensive class number to the whole of the title. Take the title "Classification in School Libraries". In the DDC the class number for classification is 025.42 and that for school libraries is 027.8. There is no provision to integrate these two numbers. Here we will have to make a choice between the two numbers. Editors usually advise us to choose the more concrete of the two, which usually comes later in the schedules. Many a time, the *order of precedence* may be given: as under 362 Social welfare problems and services at 363.1, and 364. A table of precedence is also given for Standard Subdivisions in Table 1. Choice may also depend upon the author's emphasis, or the needs of an individual library.

Similarly, a book may treat more than one subject at a time. The classifier will have to choose a generic class number if possible or give a class number for one of the subjects and ignore the others. The reason is that the DDC still aims to group documents broadly as contrasted from the faceteers' ambition to make classification an artificial language of

* S.R. Ranganathan: *Colon Classification*. 6th ed. Bombay: Asia, 1960. pp.1.7-1.8

notation translating equivalently the subject of the book into the notation used. DDC does not aim to provide a unique class number for every document in the library. Only Call Number does it.

Still another difficulty may lie for the new subjects yet not listed in the schedules. In such cases the book may be assigned to the closest possible broader class number, which may broadly cover the subject of the book. In such cases, the auxiliary tables are not added to the class number, even if the subject specially demands this. It is not done because the new edition may probably provide a specific class number by just adding a digit or two to the previous number; and the number from auxiliary tables may be added then. For example, "Teaching computers in elementary schools" was classed in 372.35 in DDC-20, as there was no separate number for computers in schools. Therefore no subdivision could be added then to that number. In the DDC-21 Computer teaching was given a separate number, viz., 372.34. Now in the DDC-22 instructions have been made more explict as to where the subdivisions are to be added or avoided. For example, see the following entry:

372.35 Science and technology
Including metric system.
Subdivisions are added
for science and technology
together, for secence alone.

It means that teaching of technology in elementary schools though placed at 372.35 will not admit further divisions. Probably in the next edition there could be a separate number for teaching of technology. For such problems the editors have provided guidance in DDC-22 Volume 1, 8.10 (p. liv).

Another important problem is the interpretation of the schedules as to the intended meaning. In spite of many notes, and cross references, it is still an elusive task. Subjectivity in interpretation can never be ruled out; and subject analysts may disagree among themselves on the connotations of a heading and on the question of assigning a correct class number to a given book.* J.B. Friis-Hansen aptly says that "identical use of DC in all countries is impossible and hardly any chance of it exists. Identical classification of the same book is a difficulty in one country, even by one person on different weekdays".** Centralised cataloguing systems such as CIP data," MARC records, WorldCat of OCLC, various national and trade bibliographies*** using the DDC help to lessen this inevitable problem to an uncertain extent. Purpose of the *Manual* in volume 1 is to promote uniformity in interpretation by different classifiers. Manual is a boon for the practical classifiers in the library.

---

* Satija, M.P. *A dictionary of knowledge organization.* Amritsar: Guru Nanak Dev University, 2004, p. 112-113.

** J.B. Friis-Hansen "What Dewey Knew" *Libri* 26(3), Sept, 1976 : 223.

*** Namely, *American Book Publishing Record* (ABPR) and the *British National Bibliography* (BNB).

3

Practical Number Building

Synthesis through "Add to..." instructions from the schedules:

1. Add to from 001 to 999
2. Add to a class number from some other small portion of the schedules.
3. Add to from the same division/section.
4. Add to through special provision (facet indicator) including the 04 General special:
5. Add from any internal table given for that class
6. Add from any of the six tables in volume 1.

Most of the specific subjects have readymade class numbers in the schedules as the DDC is basically an enumerative scheme. For some others especially multifaceted subjects the number will have to be built on a given base number. The choice of the base number is the most important step to build the desired number. S.R. Ranganathan's facet formula* is of much help in such matters, but that is no substitute to the familiarity with the DDC Schedules.

On arriving at a specific number, it may be seen, that if still required, the number may be further subdivided by some

* PMEST

number or its part as taken from the Schedules or Tables. Broadly, the above kind of additions may be divided into six categories (1-6 as above). One should, however, be careful not to build a class number which is otherwise already enumerated in the Schedules. Nor one can join two class numbers in the schedules without instructions. One general piece of advice is that the decimal point should only be put after the first three digits when the whole number has been built.

(1) ADDITION OF ANY NUMBER FROM THE WHOLE SCHEDULES 001-999 TO ANY GIVEN BASE NUMBER

One is merely required to add another whole number to given base number from the schedules. It is as easy as that.

025.46 is Library classification of specific disciplines and subjects. For library classification of any discipline one finds the instruction to add notation 001-999 to the base number 025.46. It means we are to add the class number from the schedule of that subject to the base class number 025.46, e.g., Classification of books on Mathematical analysis:

025.46 + 515 = 025.46515

(515 is the class number for Mathematical analysis)

Similarly, "Library Classification of Indian Philosophy" will get the class number:

025.46 + 181.4 = 025.461814

Similarly, 026 Libraries, archives, information centres devoted to specific subjects and disciplines is to be further subdivided like 001-999 for the class number of a library devoted to any specific subject:

Science Libraries

026+500=026.5

Terminal (or filler) zeroes are redundant in a decimal fraction; these are dropped in the ultimate class number:

Libraries of library and information science

026 + 020 = 026.02

Libraries devoted to Indian philosophy

026 + 181.4 = 026.1814

Libraries on inorganic chemistry

026 + 546 = 026.546

Similarly,

Science journalism

070.499 + 500 = 070.4495

Sports journalism

070.449 + 790 = 070.44979

331.124 Job vacancies, Openings, Opportunities

331.1241 In industries and occupations other than extractive, manufacturing, construction.

For job opportunities in the military service: to the designated base 331.1241, as per instructions, we are to add the class number of Military science taken from the schedules:

331.1241 + 355 = 331.1241355

Job opportunities in library and information science

331.1241 + 020 = 331.124102

Aptitude tests for ability in mathematics

153.94 Aptitude tests

153.94001-.94999 Tests for aptitudes in specific fields

= 153.94 + 510 (Math) = 153.9451

Aptitude test in Music

153.94 + 780 (Music) = 153.9478

Acquisition of reading materials in sciences

025.27 + 500 = 025.275

Acquisition of books on Indian history

025.27 + 954 = 025.27954

Women librarians : A Social Study

305.42 + 02 (from 020) = 305.4202

Take another example:

778.53 Motion picture photography (Cinematography) and editing

778.538 Photography of specific subjects

To the base number 778.538 we are required to add the class number from 001-999 of the subject regarding its cinematography:

Motion-picture photography of science

778.538 + 500 = 778.5385

Many more such examples can be enlisted of topics admitting further division by the whole range of the Schedules. However, this device is not to be used on is own: Classifiers may use this number building device only on invitation, though one may be tempted to use such methods on one's own initiative.

*It is quite obvious that whenever a class number admits further division from 001-999, standard subdivisions, if required for that subject, are added with three zeroes, as two zeroes may be used sometimes for a subject class number. In such cases instructions exist for addition of a standard subdivision with the required number of zeroes:

Journal of curriculum

375.0005

Similarly,

History of libraries devoted to various specific disciplines:

026.0009

---

* Read this paragraph on second reading of this book.

Archives : A journal

026.0005

(2) ADD TO A DESIGNATED BASE A PORTION OF THE CLASS NUMBER FROM SOME SMALLER AREA OF THE SCHEDULES.

Instead of admitting any whole class number from anywhere in the Schedules, a designated base may require addition from some specific part of the Schedules, from a single main class, or division or a section or even smaller than that. It is a specialised extension of the instructions Add to from 001-999. In such cases, instead of adding the whole class number to the specified base number, a portion of a number is added. Here the common digits from a series of class numbers are removed, and the digits following the generic digits are added to the designated base number. This makes the resulting class number brief, without any ambiguity in the series of the class number that such instructions yield. There can be no difficulty in the retranslation of the class number into ordinary language, too. For example:

181 Oriental philosophy

181.04-.09 [Oriental Philosophy] based on specific religions.

To derive the class number for any specified religious philosophy, we are instructed under 181.04-.09 to add the number following 29 in 294-299 to the base number 181.0 (vol. 2, p. 151). For example:

Buddhistic philosophy

The number for Buddhism is 294.3

Here the digits after 29 are "43". These are to be added to 181.0. The derived number thus is:

181.0 + 43 = 181.043

Similarly

Confucian Religion has the class number:

299.512

So Confucian philosophy will get the class number:

181.0 + 9512 = 181.09512

Let us take another example:

331.2	Compensation and other conditions of employment
331.204	In specific industries....
331.2042-.2049	In extractive, manufacturing, construction industries and occupations

For a class number for wages/condition of working in any specified industry related to manufacturing, extraction, or construction, we are required to add to the base number 331.204 the numbers following 6 in 620-690:

Wages of agricultural labour

The number for Agriculture is 630 and the digits which follow 6 are 30 to be added to the base number 331.204

Hence;

331.204 + 30 = 331.2043

Working conditions for miners

331.204 + 22 (from 622) = 331.20422

(The class number for mining being 622)

Demand for carpenters

331.123 + 94 (from 694 carpenters)

= 331.12394

Physiology of Mammals

Animal Physiology

571.1

Here we are asked to add to 571.1 the number following 59 in 590.1-599. The class number for mammals is 599. Hence the number is:

571.1 + 9 (from 599) =

571.19

Physiology of Primates

571.1 + 98 (from 599.8 Primates)

= 571.198

Some more examples:

Guides to a Christian life for members of specific denominations and sects

248.48

For specific sects, we are to add to the above base (248.48) the numbers following 28 in 280.2 – 289, e.g.:

Guides to a Puritan life

248.48 + 59 (from 285.9) = 248.4859

Guides for Methodists

248.48 + 7 (from 287) = 248.487 (Methodist is 287)

Wheat trade

381.4 [Trade in] Specific products and services

381.41 Product of Agriculture

381.413-.418 Specific products [of Agriculture]

Here we are instructed to add to the base 381.41 the number following 63 in 633-638.

For wheat the number is 633.11. Hence we will add 311 to the above designated base

381.41 + 311 (from 633.11) = 381.41311

Reviews of documents in microforms

028.13+6 (from 011.36) = 028.136

Reviews of Braille books

028.16 + 3 (from 011.63) = 028.163

---

* The first X denotes the Main class and the second a Division.

(3) "ADD TO..." FROM THE SAME DIVISION

There is a subtle difference between an "add to..." instruction from the same Division/Section, and the number being added from some remote part of the Schedules. The difference lies not in the method, but in the nature of the part of the number added. As said earlier, a Division is subdivided into Sections; second Section and its sub-divisions enumerate the action facet, while the rest of the Sections enumerate the personality facet, to speak in the Ranganathan language. These personality facets from sections XX3-XX9* are further divisible by the facets of XXI or XX2; thereby giving the general citation order as personality followed by action.* Actually it is addition of a secondary facet. One can say that this technique has made the scheme multifaceted. Take the example :

Cotton harvesting

Here cotton is the concrete subject, therefore it will form the base number. Obviously, this is a subject of agriculture; going to 630 Agriculture we find the number for Cotton at 633.51.

It is marked with an asterisk i.e.,* which at the footnote explains: "Add as instructed under 633-635". Going back to the instructions given at page 310 (vol. 3) we find a series of instructions. The very first instruction is relevant to our purpose. We are asked to add to the base (class) number the digits following 631.5 in 631.51-631.57. The class number for Harvesting is 631.55. It means that as per instructions, we are to add to 633.51 the numbers following 631.5, i.e., 5 only. Therefore, the complete class number for Cotton harvesting is

633.51 + 5 = 633.515

---

* There are exceptions to this citation order, however. For example in 571 Physiology the citation order is Action/ Entity, i.e. Physiology - Animal.

Similarly

Soil preparation for cotton

633.51 + 1 = 633.511

Cotton seeds

633.51 + 21 (from 631.521) = 633.5121

New varieties of cotton

633.51 + 23 = 633.5123

Cotton yield

633.51 + 58 = 633.5158

Cotton storing

633.51 + 68 (from 631.568) = 633.5168

Take another example:

Evolution in Porifera

Here Porifera (sponges) with the class number 593.4 will form the base number. Here we are told to add as instructed under 592-599 (p. 1186, vol.2). The instruction relevant to our purpose is 1 General topics of natural history. First we are to add 1 to the designated base number and further add the number following 591 in 591.1-591.8. In 591 the number for evolution is 591.38. Therefore, we are to add only 38 to the above compound number :

593.4 + 1 + 38 (from 591.38) = 593.4138

(Here 1 acts as a facet indicator. **The general principle that emerges is that we can add all the subdivisions of 591.3-591.7 to all the class numbers from 592-599 through a facet indicator 1.)**

Let us now find the class number for

Physical Adaptation of Invertebrates.

Processes and parts [of Invertebrates]

592

For a specific general topic, we are asked to add to 592.1 (1 being a facet indicator) the numbers following 591 in 591.3-591.7. The class number for "Physical adaptation" is 591.4.

Thus we are required to add 4 to 592.1. The complete class number, therefore, is :

592.1 + 4 (from 591.4) = 592.14

Similarly:

Physiology of Invertebrates

571.1 + 2 (from 592) = 571.12

Evolution of Invertebrates

592 + 1 + 38 (from 591.38) = 592.138

Anatomy of Invertebrates

571.3+1 (as under 571 - 572) + 2 (from 592) = 571.312

Ecology of Invertebrates

592 + 1 (from 592 - 599) + 7 (from 591.7) = 592.17

Take another example :

Chemical Reaction Kinetics of Alkaloids.

The base number for Alkaloids is 547.72.

Here, we are asked to add, as per the footnote, as instructed under 547 (on page 1029, vol .2). Since chemical kinetics is a topic of physical chemistry, the third subdivision (045 Physical chemistry) is relevant to us. Here we are instructed to add to 045 the numbers following 541.3 in 541.34-541.39.

The number for Chemical Reaction Kinetics is 541.394. The digits following 541.3 are 94 in this case. The complete class number for the title in question thus is:

547.72 + 045 + 94 (from 541.394) = 547.7204594

In this way we can extend any class number in 546 and 547. For example:

Optical properties of alkaloid solution

547.72 + 045 + 414 (from 541.3414) = 547.72045414

Thermodynamics of the chemistry of alkaloids

547.72 + 045 + 69 (from 541.369) = 547.7204569

The facet indicator for adding from the subdivisions of 541.2 is 044 as per the same instructions.

Stereochemistry of alkaloids,

547.72 + 044 + 23 (from 541.223) = 547.7204423

Quantum chemistry of alkaloids

547.72 + 044 + 8 (from 541.28) = 547.720448.

Similarly in 294.4 Jainism, specific aspects of Jainism have been placed at 294.41-294.48. These aspects can be individualised as in 201 - 209. For this we are told by the footnote to add to the base 294.4 the number following 20 in 201-209. This has been instructed under 290 (p. 261, vol. 2). Let us take an example of the Sacred Books of Jains. Our base number is 294.4 and the number for sacred books in 201-209 is 208.2. Thus to the base 294.4, we will add 82. Hence the class number for the **Sacred books of Jains** is

294.4 + 82 (from 208.2) = 294.482

Similarly:

Jain eschatology

294.4 + 23 (from 202.3) =294.423

Sacred places of Jains

294.4 + 35 (from 203.5) =294.435

Worship in Jainism

294.4 + 43 (from 204.3) = 294.443

Jain saints

294.4 + 213 (from 202.13) = 294.4213

Problems in acquisition of government publications

025.28 + 34 (from 025.3434) = 025.2834.

Collection development in Elementary school libraries

025.218 + 78222 (from 027.8222) = 025.21878222

Book selection in national libraries

025.218 + 75 (from 027.5) = 025.21875*

---

* Read this in the second round.

* (Area can also be added to 027.5)

Book selection in the Library of Congress

025.218 + 75 + 73 (Table 2) = 025.2187573

Reference service in children libraries

025.527 + 7625 (from 027.625) = 025.5277625

4-5 ADD TO ... THROUGH FACET INDICATOR

Sometimes some special subdivisions applicable to a series of numbers of a section are enumerated in the beginning of the same section. These tables of special facets are of general applicability within the same section. Instructions are provided against each subsection and their further divisions for adding to the desired facet.

Prevention of heart disease

616.12 + 05 (p. 85, vol. 3) = 616.1205*

Case histories of heart diseases

616.12 + 09 (p. 86, vol. 3) = 616.1209

Similar instructions are also found under the subdivisions of 618

618.1 Gynecology

618.11 Diseases of the ovaries

As per similar instructions one can add to this number any required facet enumerated under the heading 618.1-618.8 (p. 156-58, vol.3)

Preventive measures for ovarian diseases

618.11 + 052 = 618.11052

Surgical treatment of ovarian diseases

618.11 + 059 (p. 157, vol.3) = 618.11059

Take an example from 746 Textile arts. To many of the subdivisions of 746 may be added special subdivisions given under 746 (p. 612, vol.3); and whenever these special facets are admissible such places have been marked with an asterisk*.

In such cases, since the subject divisions have usurped the original place of the standard subdivisions, the standard subdivisions are advanced to the place beginning with a double zero:

Research in heart diseases

616.12 + 0072 = 616.120072

For instance, for a work on Crochet patterns, we find that specific class number for Crocheting is 746.434 and as per instruction we add to it the number for pattern given on page 612 (vol.3). Thus the complete class number is:

746.434 + 041 = 746.434041

Pattern in woven rugs

746.72 + 041 = 746.72041

Take an example in 546 Inorganic chemistry. Here almost all the individual elements are extendable by some special subdivisions enumerated once for all in the beginning under the general heading 546 Inorganic chemistry (p. 1021, vol. 2). The instruction here is to add to each subdivision identified by* as follows:

1 The element

2 Compounds

22 Acids and bases

24 Salts

25 Complex compounds

....

5 Physical chemistry

6 Analytical chemistry

For example, if the subject is Potassium salts, the class number for Potassium chemistry is 546.383:

Salt is a special facet having the number 24.

The complete class number for Potassium salts is

546.383 + 24 = 546.38324

Similarly, the special facet number for the physical chemistry of individual elements is 5. As per instruction, it is further divisible as the subdivisions of 541.3 as in 541.33-541.39. We are to add to 5 the digits following 541.3 in 541.33-541.39.

For example:

Physical chemistry of potassium

546.383 + 5 = 546.3835

Chemical kinetics of potassium (a topic of physical chemistry)

The base number is 546.383. Since it is the physical chemistry aspect, we add 5

546.383 + 5 = 546.3835

The digit 5 is further extendable by the subdivisions of 541.3. The class number for chemical kinetics is 541.394

Here the digits that follow 541.3 are 94. Hence the complete class number for chemical kinetics of potassium is

546.383 + 5 + 94 (from 541.394) = 546.383594.

Similarly:

Isotopes of potassium

546.383+5+ 88 (from 541.388 Isotopes) = 546.383588

Photochemistry of potassium

546.383+5+5(from 541.35 Photochemistry) = 546.38355

Quantitative analysis of sodium

546.382+61 (Quantitative analysis, p.1021 vol.2) = 546.38261

Some of the facets applicable to some of the subdivisions of 721-729: Specific aspects of architecture have been enumerated thereunder on p. 559 Volume 3.

722	Architecture from earliest times to ca.300
722.11	Ancient Chinese architecture

It, as per instruction, admits the facets enumerated under 721-729:

Drawings of ancient Chinese architecture

722.11 + 022 = 722.110222

Architectural remodeling of theatre buildings

725.822 + 0286 = 725.8220286

Architecture of buildings for the physically handicapped : An Encyclopadia

725.54 + 03 = 725.5403

6. ADD FROM ANY OF THE SIX TABLES

See chapters 5 - 10 of this book.

4

Order of Precedence

Notwithstanding the many synthetic devices in the DDC sometimes we are not able to provide a co-extensive* class number for a given complex subject having many facets. Theoretically, such facets are combinable but the DDC does not allow them to unite in a single class number.** Inevitably in such cases some facets will have to be ignored. The problem arises then as to which facet is to be chosen, and which facet ignored. *As a general rule, more specific facets are preferred over the less specific facets.* But this measure of specificity is not left to the arbitration of a classifier. Under many class numbers or centered headings, the schedules provide a precedence table that determines the priorities of the two or more class numbers; gives clear direction as to which class number is to be chosen in case of choice between two or more class numbers.***

---

* A co-extensive class number fully covers all the facets of the subject.

** (It is puzzling as to why the schedule does not allow the combination of facets especially when such situations are identified, and the feasibility and literary justification of their combination is also admitted.)

*** The table of precedence for Table 1 is discussed in the chapter on Standard Subdivisions.

In the Schedules, for example, under 155.42-155.45. Psychology of specific groupings (p. 128, vol. 2), is given the following table of precedence:

Exceptional children	155.45
Children by status, type, relationships	155.44
Children in specific age groups	155.42
Children by sex	155.43

For example, take the subject Preschool girls. Girls and preschool children are different subdivisions of 155.4, and the schedule does not provide any instruction to combine them. The two possible class numbers are:

153.423	Preschool children
153.433	Girls

As per the table of precedence given above, 155.42 and its subdivisions are to be preferred over 155.43 Children by sex. Hence the correct class number for Preschool girls is 155.423, not 155.433.

Similarly:

Psychology of gifted boys

155.45 + 5 = 155.455 (from 371.91-371.97 where gifted children is 371. 95)

Here as per the precedence table, we ignored the sex facet and further elucidated the preferred number as per instructions under 155.45 Exceptional children. *

Another table of precedence is given at 362 Social welfare problems and services (p.706, vol.2). Say we have a book on:

Providing welfare service to poor women.

Services to alleviate poverty is 362.5.

Services to women is 362.83.

As per the table of precedence under 362 the number

* In the DDC22 Priority tables also exist under 150 and 155.

362.83 is to be given precedence over 362.5. Hence the correct class number is 362.83.

Similarly:

Welfare services to politically oppressed veterans

362.87, not 362.86

Another precedence table can be found at 641.5 Cooking (p. 361, vol 3).

Vegetarian cooking for travel

641. 5636, not 641. 575

Time saving cooking for armed forces

641.57, not 641.555

Cooking breakfast for South Asians

641.57, not 641.592+914 (Table 5)

Cooking lunch in schools

641.571, not 641.53

Another table of precedence is given under 649.1 Child rearing (p 390, vol. 3)

Here instead of any priority table there is a simple instruction that of the two numbers, the number coming last in the schedules is to be preferred.

Rearing preschool girls

649.133, not 649.123

Rearing exceptional girls

649.15, and not 649.133

Rearing deaf boys

649.15+12 (dividing like 371.91-371.97)

=649.1512, not 649.132

Another table of precedence occurs at 657.1-657.9 Elements of accounting (p. 402, vol.3)

Auditing fixed assets

657.73, not 657.45

Public accounting for non-profit organisations.

657.98, not 657.61

Cost accounting in hotels and restaurants

657.837 + 0 + 42 (dividing like 657.1-657.7 as per instruction under 657.837)=657.837042, not 657.42

Book keeping in nonprofit hospitals

657.8322+0+2 (Dividing like 657.1-657.7)

=657.832202, not 657.98

A small precedence table also occurs at 747.9 Specific decorations (p. 618, vol.3)

Interior decorative lighting for weddings

747.92, not 747.93

Interior decoration with houseplants for parties

747.98, not 747.93

At 757 Paintings of human figures and their parts, a precedence table is also given (p. 626, vol .3)

Paintings of nude women

757.4 and not 757.22

Miniature portraits of men

757.7 and not 757.3

When there are no instructions, a more specific class number is given precedence over a less specific number. One mechanical formula to weigh the specificity of the two class numbers is: of the two class numbers one with a zero* and the other having no zero,** the latter is more specific, hence given precedence (Rule 5.7 (E) p. xliv, vol.1). For example:

Official status of gold coins

---

* However, one exception to this rule of zeroes occurs at 262.3-262.4 Specific form of church organization:

Government of the Roman Catholic Church

262.0 + 2 = 262.02, not 282

** This is termed as the Rule of Zero.

332.4222, not 332.42042

Political offences by the Mafia

364.131, not 364.106

Role of teachers in personal guidance programmes

371.46, not 371.4046

Team teaching in private schools

371.148 not 371.02

Wooden chairs and tables

684.13, not 684.104

Maintenance and repair of beds

684.15, not 684.1044

On the same principle, a class number with one zero will have precedence over a class number with two zeroes, and so on.

Sometimes the DDC replaces a table of precedence by a single instruction to choose an earlier or later notation (see Rule 9.6 p. lviii, vol. 1). For example, at 331.3-331.6 Labour force by personal characteristics we get the instruction (p. 422, vol. 2):

> Unless other instructions are given, class complex subjects with aspects in two or more subdivisions of this schedule in the number coming *first* in the schedules...

For example:

Labour by young women

331. 34, not 331. 4

Similarly a note could instruct us to choose the latter number as given under 305.9. Occupational and miscellaneous groups.

Sociology of unemployed doctors

305.961, not 305.906941

Sometimes the table of precedence is simply replaced by class elsewhere notes. For example, under 025 Operations of libraries, archives, information centers one reads the instruction: "Class comprehensive works on operations in specific kinds of institutions in 026-027". According to this instruction, we have for

Administration of school libraries

027.8, not 025.1

Classification in government libraries

027.5 , not 025.42

But this formula does not apply to

025.2 Collection development and acquisition

Book selection in specific types of institutions

025.218

Here one reads the instruction "Add to base number 025.218 the number following 02 in 026-027"

For example:

Book selection in school libraries

025.218 + 78 = 025.21878, not 027.8

Book selection in government libraries

025.218 + 75 = 025.21875, not 027.5

The objective of the order of precedence table, citation orders, and a host of notes especially cross reference notes, class here or elsewhere notes is to avoid cross classification and to strike maximum uniformity and standardization in the application and interpretation of the Schedules.

5

Use of Table 1: Standard Subdivisions

Information which is the predominant basis of library classification is an abstract entity. It cannot have any form by itself. It requires some physical medium for its capturing, dissemination, and preservation. A document which is a source of knowledge has always some physical form. Library classification deals with documents. Library classification, in effect, deals with knowledge as contained in documents. Therefore, library classification has to take into full account the outer and inner attributes of these physical objects embodying knowledge. It may be described by the following equation:

Library Classification = Knowledge Classification + Viewpoint of the presentation of the text + Physical attributes of the document = Subjects + Internal form + External form.

These documentary forms are both internal and external. For example, it may be expedient in a library to separate a microfilm, or a CD-ROM, from a book, though the specific subject of these three may precisely be the same. It is equally expedient to distinguish between a dictionary and a periodical of a subject; as well as the philosophical viewpoint from the historical one of the same subject. To account for such physical attributes of the documents, Melvil Dewey in the second edition of the scheme (1885) separated such non-subject forms of the documents and listed them in the beginning of each division. These tables can be attached to any class number and always remain the same in name and notation. The notation for such recurring concepts always starts with a zero and has a meaning only when attached to some class; it cannot be used independently. **These are called "standard" because their meaning and notation remain the same wherever these are used.*** What started truly as "form divisions" have evolved (with the complexities and varieties of incoming documents) to an agglomeration of some complex but recurring concepts termed as standard subdivisions. The standard subdivisions as they stand today in DDC22 (Volume 1, pp. 185-214) may broadly be categorized as under:

01 ; parts of 02, 07, and 09	Viewpoints
02 partially, 03, 05 and 06	Physical (Bibliographic) forms of the treatment of subjects
04, 08 and to some extent 09	Facet indicators to introduce a new facet.

These have been divided into five kinds A/E in the Manual (vol. 1, pp, 5-199). The scope of the standard subdivisions has been widened so much that it is better to go through

* These were termed as form divisions, as mostly these stood for the forms of the documents. In the second edition they were listed at the beginning of each of the 100 Divisions. Therefore, the general form a class number took was XXO.1-9, as said earlier. In the succeeding editions the table of form divisions was expanded, and given in a table at the beginning of the schedules. In the seventeenth edition these form divisions were renamed to "standard subdivisions", as the recurring non-subject divisions gathered there had obviously outgrown the form divisions. Now, these include some recurring viewpoints, and even facet indicators as they stand now.

Table 1 (in volume 1) to know their scope and variety. Knowledge of their nature and scope will surely add to the efficiency of classifiers. Rules for adding standard subdivisions to a class number have been provided in Sections 8.3 to 8.10 of the Introduction to the Dewey Decimal Classification in Volume 1 (p. lii-liv). Here rules are given on how to use Table 1. Some brief instructions to apply them and the order of preference also precede the core Table 1. A great many instructions regarding standard subdivisions are found in the Manual on (pp. 5-19, vol. 1). Rules for adding an ss are summarized as follows:

1. A Standard subdivision is added to the ultimate schedule number of the document in question. Having reached the most specific class number, *we do not necessarily need an invitation to add a standard subdivision from Table 1.*

   Encyclopaedia of Islam

   297 + 03 = 297.03

   (Here Islam is the subject and encyclopaedia a standard subdivision).

   Encyclopedia of the Holy Koran

   297.12203

   History of the Ahmadiya movement

   297.86 + 09 = 297.860 9

   (We have added ss 03 and 09, though there are no instructions to do so at these class numbers).

2. Subjects whose specific class numbers do not yet exist in the schedules should not be expanded with a standard subdivision.

   For example:

   Standards for goat's milk

Standards is an ss whose number is-0218 in Table 1. Goat's milk is a subject of animal husbandry. Milk production is 637.14 (which is cow's milk). All other kinds of milk are put under 637.17 with no further subdivision. Consequently, no specific class number has been provided for goat's milk. Therefore, as per the rules, we cannot add standard subdivisions here; the correct class number, therefore, is 637.17, and not 637.170218. This is done not because of any structural difficulty; it is an advice to ease expansion in future. May be some future edition provides a number for goat's milk, which probably would be a subdivision of 637.17. If any ss is added to 637.17 it may entail total effacing and rewriting when we provide co-extensive class number in conformity with some future edition. Moreover, to assign a standard subdivision to a number implies that the subdivision applies to the entire contents of the number; you mislead when you assign a standard subdivision to a part of a class.

3. **Usually two standard subdivisions are not applied in succession to** a class number. If a subject poses two standard subdivisions, then only one is to be applied, on preferential basis, and the other is to be ignored. A table of preference is prefixed to the Table 1. If we examine, the preferential order, it becomes obvious that facet indicator General Special is followed by viewpoints, and the real form divisions come in the end. It means *internal forms are to be preferred over the external forms.* However, in Table 1 - 093-099, there are provisions for adding standard subdivisions to standard subdivisions.

Let us take the example "Encyclopaedia of Organisations on Applied Psychology". Here encyclopaedia and organisation both are ss with the notations 03 and 06, respectively. Only one of them is to be added. As per the Precedence table, 06 is to be given preference over 03. Therefore, the correct class number is 158.06, *not* 158.03 or any number combining the two ss, viz., 158.0306

Similarly, a Directory of Library Schools in India will get the class number

020.71154 instead of 020.2554

Therefore, whenever two standard subdivisions seem applicable to a work, this table may be consulted to know which of them is to be applied, and which is to be ignored, when all things are equal. When one standard subdivision concept is being stressed or is clearly more important, it is used no matter what the preference table says.

IRREGULARITIES

At some places in the schedules the standard subdivision are already attached to a class number. Most of these are given a variant meaning to suit a local situation. Meanings of some of the ss are locally extended.

Extension in Meaning

If any of the ss when applied to a class gets some local name in that context, then in that schedule all such proper standard subdivisions are to be used. In all such cases, the notation is compatible with Table 1, but the nomenclature is somewhat modified. The ss 011 Value in the context of 331 Labour economics has been given the extended meaning: "Freedom, dignity, value of labour" and denoted as 331.013.

An extended meaning of ss 01 Philosophy and theory exists in the Main Class 700 Theater, Fine and decorative arts

701 Philosophy and theory of fine and decorative arts.

701.1 Appreciative aspects

701.17 Aesthetics

701.18 Criticism and appreciation

Classifiers should abstain from giving homemade extended meanings to standard subdivisions, whatsoever the situation be, and howsoever apt the self-extended meaning may appear to be.

Irregular Places

Some standard subdivisions are shown as subject divisions and consequently moved to a division in the array. It happens because that compound subject has a subject value and considerable literary warrant. Such treatment allows the further extension of such subjects. This happens usually for the geographical and historical treatment of a subject:

331 Compensation [for Labour]

331.29 Historical, geographical, persons treatment of compensation (instead of 331.209).

To avoid cross classification cross references, class else where notes are provided from a probable class number likely to be looked at by the classifier to the actual number used in the Schedules. For example, in the above case, the not used class number [331.2109] is enclosed in square brackets, and a cross reference directs the classifier to 331.29. Similarly, Techniques, apparatus, material for art metal work is 739.1 instead of 739.028, as techniques, apparatus, etc is an ss but here it has been enumerated like a subject.

Similarly, 720.9 is Historical, geographical, persons treatment of architecture. But the architectures of specific Ages, instead of being provided in 720.901-905 have been shifted to 722-724. Accordingly at [720.901-905] one reads the instructions "Do not use, class in 722-724." Therefore:

Medieval architecture

723 instead of 720.902

Twentieth century architecture

724.6 instead of 720.904

Another interesting aberration occurs at 666.3 Pottery-Ceramic technology. Here, we are told to add ss at 666.31-39, instead of at the usual place 666.301-309. Thus a **Journal of pottery will get the class number 666.35, and Teaching and study of pottery will be 666.37,** and so on.

Some other irregularities also occur in the case of the use of the chronological periods in Table 1. In usual cases any chronological period division is to be taken from the Table 1, where the ss 09 has been further subdivided as 0901-0905, enumerating all segments of history. These are obviously attachable to any class number, but for some classes, (for example, 700 Arts, 800 Literature and 900 History) some special period tables have been provided. Therefore, in such cases these tables are to be used, instead of the general one in ss 090. In fact, in the case of main classes 800 and 900, the period is a subject facet, instead of being merely a time auxiliary. For example:

20th Century English poetry

821.91 instead of 821.0904

Elizabethan English drama

822.3 instead of 822.09031

History of India in the 1970's

954.05 instead of 954.09047 or even 954.047

England under Elizabeth I

942.055 instead of 942.09031

History of 18th century Germany

943.05 instead of 943.09033

One more interesting irregularity occurs in 340. The usual place for ss here is given as 340.02-09. For example:

Dictionary of law

340.03

Study and teaching of law

340.07

But the philosophy and theory of law has been placed at 340.1 with its own extended meaning:

340.112 Law and ethics

340.115 Law and society

Extending the irregular use of the standard subdivisions a bit further, we find numerous cases where a geographical facet is made inherent in the structure of the class number. In such cases, the geographical facet is not added through the ss 09. For instance:

General statistics of Europe
314 instead of 310.94

General statistics of France
314.4 instead of 310.944

General statistics of India
315.4 instead of 310.954

At times, a standard subdivision is redundant if the form or viewpoint is inherent in the subject itself:

Dictionary of the English language
423 instead of 420.3 or 423.03

History of India
954 instead of 954.009

Examples of this kind may be multiplied without end.

Enigma of Zeroes

In Table 1 every ss begins with a zero, which is essentially a facet indicator marking the transition from subject division to form division in the class number. The original rules for adding standard subdivisions (though quite simple and uniform in the beginning) have become rather complex in the face of the warping structure of the DDC. Sometimes a featured zero may seem missing, while at others an ss may begin with one, two, or even three zeroes. This has happened to accommodate new subjects. These oddities have been abruptly grafted rather than evolved. Some subjects have been prepositioned to usurp the hereditary place of standard subdivisions. For example, 344.05 is not a journal of Social law 344. It is the subject division connoting Police services.

Similarly, 616.07 is not the study and teaching of diseases, but means pathology.

Since the place for standard subdivisions has been occupied by subject divisions in such cases, the standard subdivisions are so designated as to distinguish them from subject divisions to avoid confusion. This is done by denoting the ss with two zeroes or three zeroes as the case may be. Hence, there is no fixed formula for attaching or identifying an ss. *The only formula is to follow the instructions, if any, provided in the Schedules under every class member.* In all such abnormal cases, the instructions are invariably provided sufficiently. Such irregularities have discounted a great deal the mnemonic value of the scheme, and consequently the efficiency too has been at a stake.

Dictionary of human diseases

616.003

Philosophy and theory of constitutional law

342.001

Journal of constitutional law

342.005

Encyclopaedia of Indian history

954.003

Special subdivisions of standard subdivisions

Some of the standard subdivision such as 08, 0901-0905, and 093-099 have their own table of special subdivisions which can be added to their asterisked subdivisions. For example, under-08 (p.22, vol.1) the subdivisions are applicable to its entire range of subdivisions. These are subdivisions of subdivisions. In fact this results in the use of two standard subdivisions simultaneously:

Statistics on the reading habits of children

028.9 (Reading habits) + 083 (T1; children) + 021 (Stat.

spl. sub. div under - 08 (T1,))=028.9083021

Reading habits of teenager girls in India

028.9 + 08352 (T1; teenager girls) + 09 (spl. sub div under-08 (T1,)) + 54 (T2; as instructed under 09)

= 028.908352 0954

Museums of ancient Buddhism in Japan

294.3+ 0901 (T1,) + 074 (spl. subdivision) + 52 (T2)

= 294.3090107452

Similarly under T1-093-099 there is a table of special subdivisions (p. 214, vol.1) which can be added to all its subdivisions.

Statistics on publishing in India

070.59 + 09 (T1) + 54 (T2) + 02 (Spl. subdivision)

= 070.59095402

Museum of Indian Dolls in the UK

745.59221 + 09 (T1) + 54 (T2) + 074 (Spl. subdivision)

+41(T2;UK) = 745.59221095407441

Rules for Adding Standard Subdivisions

Subject to the above rules, a standard subdivision may be added to any class number. If the ultimate class number is a Main class having two zeroes or Division having one zero, then these **filler zeroes are removed while adding the standard subdivision.*** For example, take the title "Encyclopaedia of Science". Science is 500, and Encyclopaedia is a ss with notation 03. Since in 500 there are two filler zeroes, these are to be removed. The synthesised class number is:

500+03 = 5ϕϕ + 03 = 503

Similarly,

---

* There are many exceptions to this rule.

Journal of philosophy

100+05=1ϕϕ + 05 = 105

In 510, Mathematics, we have only one filler zero, so, it is to be removed while adding any standard subdivision:

History of mathematics

510+09=51ϕ + 09 = 510.9

Philosophy of mathematics

510+01=51ϕ+01=510.1

The reader may be reminded here that zero/zeroes removed are those not belonging to the ss but to the class number. The featured zero of the ss is always there.

These statutory zeroes are not to be removed, or removed only partially, as the occasion may demand, if the subject divisions have been moved to the places of ss. For example

Dictionary of social sciences

300.3 and not 303

Here only one zero has been removed, though there are two redundant or filler zeroes in 300 social sciences. This has been done because the class number 303 has already been assigned the meaning of Social process, in Sociology. Similarly, 532.005 is a Journal of fluid mechanics instead of 532.05, which means dynamics here. Here (under 532) instructions have been provided to use ss as 532.001-532.009. Such instructions do not have hierarchic force, i.e., ss to the subdivisions of 532 are to be added with normal zeroes, as there will be no ambiguity.

Journal of dynamics

532.0505 instead of 532.05005

Research in statics

532.02072 instead of 532.020072

Here are given examples to illustrate the variety and scope of standard subdivisions.

Apparatus and equipment for circulation services in a library

025.6028

Library and information science profession

020.23

A dictionary of Acronyms in library and information science

020.148, not 020.3

(By applying Table of preference given in T1 (p. 186, vol. 1)

Indian history through pictures

954.00222

History of Mughal India through pictures

954.0250222

A Video on the DDC

025.4310208

A Video on the history of the DDC

025.43109, not 025.4310208

History of the DDC up to the end of the 19th century

025.43109034

Exercises in the DDC

025.431076

*Many of the standard subdivisions may be further extended by synthesis either through Tables 2, 5, 6, 7, or from the Schedules :

Optical principles of coordinate and post-coordinate indexing

025.484+015(T1) +35 (from the class number 535 light and paraphotic phenomena)

025.48401535

Here 015 Scientific principles is a standard subdivision

---

* Please read this paragraph on second reading of this book.

which is to be further divided like 510-590; and Optics is 535.

Indian Library Association

020.622+54 (Table 2) =020.62254

The class number for a national library organisation is 020.622 to which area notation from Table 2 is to be added as per instructions.

Universities imparting library science education in Maharashtra State.

020.711+5479 (T2)=020.7115479

Under T1-07 education -0711 is an ss standing for college and universities which is further extendable by area.

Research in library classification in Canada

025.42+072+0+71=025.42072071

Life of Melvil Dewey by Fremont A. Rider

020.92

Autobiography of S R Ranganathan

020.92

Dictionary of philosophy

100+03=103

History of philosophy in India

100+09+54=109.54

(It is not the history of Indian philosophy). Here the ss 09 has been extended by the Area Table.

Reader advisory services to doctors

025.54+088+61=025.5408861=025.5408861

Here, the subject has been treated with respect to doctors (a non-ethnic, regardless of national groups of people). Here ss 088 has been extended by 011-999 where medical science is 610.

Reading interests of Physicians

028.9+088+61(from 610 schedules)=028.908861

but

Reading interests of children

028.55

Here the use of ss 08 for children will be redundant, as the class number itself means children.

Reading habits of Indians (national group)

028.9+089+91411(Table5)=028.908991411

089 is the ss for treatment of the subject among national groups, which is to be further extended by the Table 5, where the number for Indians is 91411. The use of ss 088 and 089 should be distinguished from -024 which means a work for specific type of users.

Science for social scientists

500 + 024 (T1) + 300 = 502.43

Mathematical statistics for librarians

519.502402 i.e., 519.5 + 024 (T1) +02 (from 020 schedules)

Arithmetic for managers

513.024658

Political conditions of the world in the 21st century: A forecast

320+0905 (T1) + 01 (special Table under ss-08 on p. 202 vol. 1)

= 320.90501 (one filler zero has been removed)

Political conditions of India in the 21st century

320.95405

Marxian economics in the 1950s

335.409045

Marxian economics in the USSR in the 1950s

335.4+09(T1) + 47(T2) + 045 (from 09045 Table 1)
=335.40947045

6

Use of Table 2: Geographical Areas, Historical Periods, Persons

Whenever a subject is studied within the context of a given geographical area, the ultimate class number is qualified by the area number taken from Table 2. In some subjects such as general statistics, history, the area is already embedded in the class number. For example, 315 General statistics of Asia. Here the digit 5 is for Asia. The need to add area notation usually occurs in the social sciences and the humanities where the treatment and practice of a subject varies from place to place. Some other disciplines may also need the area facet occasionally. Where the schedule does not authorize us to add from the area table, the area table can still be added through ss 09 from Table 1.

This is largest of all the auxiliary tables (pp. 215 to 615 out of the total of 528 pages devoted to all the six tables); the largeness consists not in any variety of subdivisions as it is in details. A brief paragraph of instructions (p. 215 precedes the enumeration of area numbers. All areas of the world, natural geographical divisions, or political or administrative units, or some scattered geophysical divisions of the earth or some noncontiguous conceptual divisions based on various characteristics of people who habitat them, have been accommodated in divisions 1 to 9. The area 1 stands for the scattered regions bound by some geophysical characteristic or by some social characteristic, e.g., plane regions, forests, deserts, oceans, socio-economic regions, and so on. The digit 2 has been allotted to persons regardless of area, region, places. Notation 3 denotes the ancient world; and the modern world as divided into various continents has been denoted by notations 4 to 9. Obviously the details for the geographical subdivisions of area numbers for the USA 73-79 are far more deep than those of any other country. Here subdivisions have been enumerated down to county, and even city level, whereas for many countries, there are no further divisions at all.

The area number is added to the ultimate class number, though some classes are directly based on the geographical characteristic, so the number for area is inherent there; for example, in history 954 is the history of India, 973 is history of the USA, as-54 and -73 are area numbers as taken from the area table; similarly 314 is general statistics of Europe and 315 is general statistics of Asia, where 4 and 5 respectively are the area numbers of Europe and Asia.

Use of Table 2 for area does not pose any difficulty. Whenever a class number needs extension by geographical area, there are sufficient instructions in the schedules to do so. Occasionally, a division (usually at 9 in the array) is left for geographical and historical treatment of the subject:

Political conditions

320.9

(As per instructions, this class number is to be further subdivided by the area numbers 1 to 9 from Table 2)

Political conditions of India

320.954 i.e., 320.9 + 54 (T2)

Political conditions in Rajasthan

320.9+544(T2) = 320.9544

Political conditions in the USA

320.973

Political conditions in Christian countries

320.91761 i.e., 320.9 + 1761 (T2)

Sometimes a class number itself is to be directly divided by the area number:

Constitutional law of Canada

342+71 (T2) = 342.71

Japanese Diet

328+52 (T2) = 328.52

Foreign policy of Britain

327+41(T2) = 327.41

Here class numbers 342, 328, and 327 have been divided by the area numbers 71, 52, and 41 respectively.

Adding Area without Instruction:

Where there are no instructions but the subject of the document under classification requires the addition of an area number from Table 2, then the area number is added to the class number via ss 09. Latter works as a facet indicator:

Child labour in India — an economic study

331.31 + 09 (T1) + 54 (T2) = 331.310954

Men's costumes in the Himachal Pradesh

391.1095452 i.e., 391.1 + 09 (T1) + 5452 (T

Freedom of speech in Communist countries

323.443+09+1717(T2) 323.443091717

Standard of living in rural areas

339.47+09+1734(T2) = 339.47091734

INFLIBNET (India)

004.678 + 09 + 54 (T2) = 004.6780954

So, an area number may be added to any class number by either of the two ways depending upon whether there is an invitation or not to add from the area table.

Adding Area through 0 only

Sometimes, an area number may be added through 0 instead of 09. For example, at 920.03-.09 biographies by specific geographical areas.

Biographies of persons living in India

920+0+54(T2) = 920.054

Here, as per instructions, the area number 54 for India has been added to the base number 920.0

Biographies of persons living in Rajasthan

920.0544

General libraries in the USA

027.073

General libraries in Pennsylvania

027.0748

If a subject is a study extending to two non-adjacent areas, we cannot add area numbers for both; we will have to choose one.

Democracy in India and the USA

321.80954 or 321.80973

If, however, there is an interaction between two different areas, then the Schedules *sometimes* provides a mechanism to join them:

Foreign relations between India and the USA

327.54+0+73=327.54073

Here, as per instructions, the class number 327 is to be subdivided by the first area, then 0 is to be added and to the result the area number for the second geographical area is to be added.

Similarly,

India's foreign policy towards non-aligned countries

327.54+0+1716=327.5401716

Trade agreements between India and the USA

382.954073 = 382.9 + 54 (T2) + 0 +73 (T2)

Migration from India to the USA

304.8+73(T2)+0+54(T2)=304.873054

Migration from Asia to Europe

304.8 + 4 + 0 + 5 = 304.8405

Country of destination is the first facet and the country of origin in the last facet.

Cases where Area is already a Part of the Class Number :

Sometimes, a geographical facet is inherent in the subject, therefore, it appears, as a subject division in the class number:

History of India

954

General statistics of Asia

315

In such cases, these class numbers can further be divided like the area table to provide class numbers in respect of subordinate areas.

History of Rajasthan*

954.4

General statistics of India*

315.4

General statistics of Rajasthan *

315.44

---

* More such examples are given in Chapter 13 of this book.

(544 is the number for Rajasthan in Table 2)

A class number extended by an area notation can also admit a chronological subdivision. In such cases, we are only required to add the subdivision of 09 in 0901-0905 from Table 1 or by the special chronological subdivisions, if provided:

History of Mughal India

954.025

History of Rajasthan under the Mughals

9+544(T2)+025(from 954.025) = 954.4025

Historical and geographical treatment of science

509

History of science in India

500+09(T1)=54(T2) =509.54

Two zeroes in 500 have been dropped in the final synthesis

History of science in British India

509.5403

Here the chronological subdivision 03 has been taken from ss 090.

General statistics of Asia in the 19th Century

315.034

Here 034 stands for the 19th century, as taken from the chronological table of standard subdivisions.

Political conditions in India in the 1980s

320.954048

Political conditions in Rajasthan in the 1980s

320.9544048

Sometimes, an area may be further extended by the special subject divisions as in the cases of 340 Law and 350 Public Administration:

* More such examples are given in Chapter 13 of this book.

Military, tax, trade, industrial law

343

Income tax law

343.052

Indian income tax law

343 + 54 (T2) + 052 (from 343.052)

=343.54052

(see instruction under 093-099 of 342-347, p. 547, vol.2)

Here 343 has first been divided by country (India-54) then the resulting class number has been further extended by the subject division 052 Income tax of 343.

Similarly:

Law of public health

344.04

Indian law of public health

344.5404

US law of public health

344.7304

Prime minister (in the cabinet form of government)

352.23

The prime minister of India

352.230954

Queen of Britain

352.2330941

Separate provision of the area table since the 17th edition has made possible the division of the earth and population clusters from various conceptual viewpoints. These are various physiogeographic and socio-economic regions, all shown as subdivisions of 1:

Standard of living in villages

339.47+09+1734(T2)=339.47091734

Atmospheric pressure in Mountains

551.54+09+143=551.5409143

Here 143 is mountains from the Area table added through the ss 09.

As per instructions given under -1 (Table 2, p.36, vol 1) each subdivision of the 1 area has the option to be qualified by any country 3-9 from the same area table. This can increase the versatility of the scheme:

Standard of living in Indian villages

339.47+09+1734(T2)+0+54(T2)=339.47091734054

339.47+09+1734(T2)+0+54(T2)=339.47091734054

Atmospheric pressure in Indian mountains

551.54+09+143(T2)+0+54(T2)=551.5409143054*

Political conditions in Communist countries

320.91717

Political conditions in communist countries of Asia*

320.9+1717(T2)+0+5(T2)=320.9171705

Political conditions in Christian countries of Africa*

320.9+1761(T2)+0+6(T2)=320.9176106

Here all the subdivisions of 1 have been further extended by the area number from 3-9 via 0 which acts as a facet indicator. **Bear in mind, however, these five examples are optional, not standard.**

Use of T2 with other Tables

Some of the divisions may further be subdivided by some of the other auxiliary tables. For example -174 Regions where specific ethnic, national groups predominate: obviously this number is further divisible by the auxiliary Table 5:

Places where Punjabi people predominate

174(T2)+9142(T5)=–1749142

---

* This has been done as per option under - 1 (T2) p 217, vol. 1.

Social status of women in the regions where Punjabi people predominate

305.42+09+1749142=305.42091749142

Similarly, division -175 Regions where specific languages predominate:

Reading habits in English-speaking countries

028.9+09+175 (Table 2)+21 (Table 6)

=028.90917521

Here area division 175 (added via 09) has been further divided by Table 6, where the number for the English language is 21.

Hospitality of Punjabi people

395.3+09(T1)+175(T2)+9142(T_6)=395.3091759142

Here area 175, added via 09, has been extended by Table 6, where 9142 is the number for the Punjabi language.

Similarly, area 176 can be further extended by religion as taken from 29 and its subdivisions in the schedules:

School discipline in Muslim countries

371.5+09+176 (Table 2)+7 (From 297 schedules, vol. 2)

=371.5091767

Here to 176 we have added the digits following 29, in 292-299 where the number for Islam is 297.

Restricted range of Area Numbers to be Added

In the schedules many a time instructions specify to "add areas notation 3-9 from Table 2". It only means that the areas denoted by the subdivisions 1 and 2 fall outside the jurisdiction of such instructions. In such cases, we cannot add directly areas from subdivisions 1 and 2 (Table 2). If needed we can add such class numbers via the ss 09. For example, Foreign policy of non-aligned nations *cannot have the following number*:

327.1716

The correct number is 327.091716

Similarly,

Parliaments in non-aligned nations

328.091716

Civil rights in Communist countries

323.091717

7

Use of Table 3: Subdivisions for the Arts, for Individual Literatures, for Specific Literary Forms

As the name of this auxiliary table implies, this table is mostly meant for the main class 800 Literature.* Since the 20th edition Table 3 has been divided into three subtables, viz, 3A, 3B, and 3C.

Table 3A is for works by or about individual authors.

Table 3B is for works by or about more than one author.

Table 3C is to be used in conjunction with Table 3B and in 808-809.

It may be pointed out that the subdivisions enumerated in these three Tables are not new or unfamiliar. These three tables make easy the mode of addition of facets without increasing their scope.

---

* This table was introduced, along with other tables, for the first time in the 18th edition (1971), and has since considerably eased the number building process in this class which has always been considered a problematic area to some extent.

Table 3A is the simplest of the three tables since **individual authors are permitted only the facets of literary form and period.** Table 3B is far more complicated.

Table 3B consists of the Standard Subdivisions in conformity with Table 1. Here the ss-08 can be further extended by Table 3C. The ss 09 'History, description, critical appraisal' is applicable to the body of literature regardless of form or language in which the literature is written. The ss 09 is extendable either by the period tables, or by some literary viewpoints taken from Table 3C but not by both, if no form of literature is given. **It may be noted that time period is to be taken not from Table 1, as each language literature has its own special period tables.** Therefore, both standard subdivisions 08 and 09 are somewhat modified forms of the standard subdivisions here. The hard core of the table consists of the various forms of literature, which are the same for every literature irrespective of the language in which it is written:

-1 Poetry

-2 Drama

-3 Fiction

-4 Essays

-5 Speeches

-6 Letters

-7 Satire and humour

-8 Miscellaneous writings

Each form subdivision has further been subdivided into its various kinds and further into varieties, if any. These

---

* In case of ss 08, its pristine meaning (that it carried up to the 18th edition) has been preserved, i.e., it still denotes collections and anthologies whereas for other main classes ss 08 no more stands for anthologies, etc. Hence it is now a more or less a special standard subdivisions for 800 Literature.

scopes/ kinds/ varieties of forms have been further subdivided through a single zero, and the ss are also applicable to the form divisions through double zeroes. For example, take the form division 3 Fiction:

-3001-3009	Standard subdivisions; collection; history, description, critical appraisal
-301-308	Fiction of specific scopes and kinds
-301	Short stories
-308	Specific kinds of fiction
-3081	Historical and period fiction
-3083	Sociological, psychological, realistic fiction
-3085	Love and romance
-3087	Adventure fiction

31-39 is fiction of specific periods. Bare (unextended) form divisions 1-8 are divisible by the period divisions specific to each language literature. Kinds of form do not admit period facet. Take, for example the case of English fiction:

- 31 Fiction of Early English Period
- 32 Fiction of Pre-Elizabethan Period
- 33 Fiction of Elizabethan Period
- 34 Fiction of Post-Elizabethan Period
- 35 Fiction of Queen Anne Period
- 36 Fiction of Later 18th Century
- 37 Fiction of early 19th Century
- 38 Fiction of Victorian Period
- 39 Fiction of 20th Century

Similarly, for, say, Hindi fiction the periods are as follow:

- 31 Hindi Fiction upto 1345
- 32 Hindi Fiction from 1345-1645
- 33 Hindi Fiction from 1645-1845

- 34 Hindi Fiction from 1845-1895
- 35 Hindi Fiction from 1895-1920
- 36 Hindi Fiction from 1920-1940
- 37 Hindi Fiction after 1940
- 372 Hindi Fiction of 21st Century

After the period division, we can further add the special ss as given in Table 3B.

Main class 800 has many facets, viz., language, form, period, standard subdivision, the latter being further extendable by a variety of viewpoints or topics. In view of the multiplicity of facets, their citation order presents some complications especially when not all the facets are present. Language, form, and period are the core facets in their decreasing order of importance. Let us discuss the various cases one by one.

I. When the language facet is absent

The study of literature in general falls in the sections 801 to 809. It is clear that these are the standard subdivisions (of course modified) as applied to the bare main class:

801 Philosophy and theory [of Literature]

802 Miscellany

803 Dictionaries, encyclopaedias, etc.

805 Serial publications

806 Organisations

807 Education, research, related topics

808 Rhetoric and collections of literary texts from more than one literature

809 History, description, critical appraisal of more than one literature.

Subdivisions of 801 and part of 808 have been enumerated in the schedules; some synthesis is also possible here. However, the citation order in 808.8 "Collections of literary texts from more than one literature" needs some illustrations. The citation formula is

Base number 808.8+form+period (from Table 1)

Collections from 20th century literature (regardless of form and language)

808.8001-.8005 Collections from specific periods.

As per instructions here, we are to add to the base number 808.800, the number following 090 in 0901-0905 from Table 1 (of standard subdivisions). The number for the 20th century is 0904, thus the digit following 090 is "4" only. Hence the class number is

808.800+4=808.8004

Similarly:

Collection of 17th century literature

808.800+31=808.80031

Selections from literature of the 1970s

808.800+47=808.80047

Collections of poetry

808.81

Collections of poetry from the 1970s

808.81+0+47=808.81047

808.81 is collections of poetry. This number is an asterisked number. As per instructions given under 808.81-808.88 (p. 767, vol.3) we have added to 808.81 the notation for period as explained there. Again the period has been taken from the general period table, viz, Table 1 Standard subdivisions. As a rule, **when no language is given, the time period is to be taken from Table 1.**

It may be noted that period division now can be added to the collections of some specific forms of literature or displaying some specific feature.

Collection of epic poetry of the 20th century

808.81 + 32 (from 1032 T3B) + 09

as given under 102 - 107 (p.628, vol. 1) + 00904 (T3C)

= 808.81320900904

Collection of 20th century one act plays

808.82+41 (from 2041 T3B) + 09 (As mentioned under -102-107 (T3B)) + 00904 (T3C)

(-00901-00905 T3C, p. 64, vol. 1)

= 808.82410900904

II. When the language facet is present

Literatures of specific languages are placed in 810-890, and the language makes the first facet in the citation order. An introduction to the procedure for building a class number for any language literature has been explained in the schedules on pages v3:773 and fully at the beginning of Tables 3A and 3B and in the Manual, vol. 1, pp 23-38.

A combination of main class digit 8 and the language constitutes the compound facet, which is termed as the base number. It is the base to which all other facets are added in an ordained order. Base numbers for almost all the languages have been enumerated and specifically indicated. For certain languages, this base number can be built with the help of language numbers taken from Table 6 Languages:

For example:

891 .99	Other Indo-European literatures
891.991	Albanian
891.892	Armenian
891. 993-.998	Other.

Here the instruction reads: Add to 891 .99 the numbers following -9199 in notation 91993-91998 from Table 6, e.g., Hittite 891 .998 (from 91998 Hittite Table 6). In this way, the class number for Tocharian language literature is 891.994. Similarly 891.991 is Albanian literature (from 91991 Table 6).

These numbers can further be extended by Table 3A.

To the available base number in the schedules, we add the facets in the following order :

Base number+form [Table 3A] +period + ss 08 or 09 (Subject/viewpoint from Table 3B) +T3C

It is obvious that in a given literary work all the above facets may not be present all the time. Whenever Tables 3A or 3B are to be used, such base numbers are marked with an asterisk. For major literatures readymade class numbers adding the form facet have been enumerated.

For example:

821 English poetry

822 English drama

827 English satire and humor

861 Spanish poetry

862 Spanish drama

863 Spanish fiction

864 Spanish essays

865 Spanish speeches

866 Spanish letters

867 Spanish satire and humor

868 Spanish miscellaneous writings

Instructions to use Tables 3A and 3B to construct a class number have been explained in a programmatic manner preceding the Tables. These instructions have made the facet structure quite transparent, though the instructions do not make very easy reading mostly due to the multiplicity of facets and various means of applying them :

In the case of individual authors the standard

subdivisions and their further extension by Tables 3B and 3C is not admissible. For individual author the formula is

Base + T3A + Period (from Schedules)

Hence books by and on an individual author get the same number.

For example:

A critical study of John Keats's poetry

(He was an English poet of the early 19th century)

82 (Base) + 1 (Form Poetry) +7 (Period from v3:777)

= 82 + 1 + 7 = 821.7

(Here we cannot add the ss for criticism.)

Similarly a study of plot construction in the novels of Thomas Hardy will get the class number as follows:

82 (Base) +3 (Form, Fiction from Table 3A) + 8 (Period from v3 : 777)

=82+3+8=823.8

Here, the critical element Plot construction will have to be ignored. **Any work of fiction by Hardy or any work on Hardy as a fiction writer will get the class number 823.8.** Not only this the various Victorian novelists, such as Hardy, George Eliot, Thackery, Dickens, and Mrs. Gaskell can only be differentiated through book numbers as they all will get the same class number 823.8.

III. In case the form facet is absent: In works by or about more than one author (Table 3B) the citation formula takes the following order:

For collections of works with a specific theme :

Base Number+080(T3B)+Table 3 C

Here Table 3A is absent.

For critical studies :

Base Number+0900+Period for that specific literature; or

Base number +09+Table 3C for theme or viewpoint.

A Collection of Hindi literature with love theme

891.43+080(T3B)+354(T3C)=891.43080354

Collection of Hindi literature on tragedy and horror

891.43+080+16 (T3C)=891.4308016

Critical study of characters in English literature

82+09(T3B)+27(T3C)=820.927

History of 20th century English literature

82+0900(T3B)+91 (from p. 777, vol.3)=820.90091

In the facet formula, the third facet is the time period in which the author flourished as a writer. It may be noted that in the case of a specific language literature, the period is not to be taken from ss 09 of Table 1. For every language literature special period divisions enumerating epochs of that particular literature have been given in the Schedules (Vol. 3) at the beginning of each language literature. For example, for Modern Indian Literatures the period table given under 891.4 is:

1	Early period to 1345.
2	1345-1645
3	1645-1845
4	1845-1895
5	1895-1919
6	1920-1939
7	1940-
71	1940-1999
72	2000-

One thing more to be noted about the period table is that in case the literature in that language is written in more than one country, then different period tables are given for each major country. For example, for French literature different period tables exist for Asian and African countries, for Belgium, for Canada and, of course, for France. Their necessity is obvious, as each country has different epochs in its literary history. For instance, for French language literature the period table for French is:

For Asian and African Countries

1	Early period to 1959
2	1960-199
3	2000-

For Belgium

1	Early Period to 1829
2	1830-1899
3	1900-1999
32	1900-1945
34	1945-1999
4	2000-

For Canada

3	Colonial period to 1867
4	1867-1899
5	1900-
52	1900-1945
54	1945-1999
6	2000-

For France

1	Early period to 1399
2	1400-1499
3	Renaissance period, 1500-1599
4	Classical period, 1600-1715
5	18th Century, 1715-1789
6	1789-1815
7	Constitutional monarchy, 1815-1848
8	1848-1899
9	1900-

91 1900-1999

912 Early, 1900-1945

914 Later, 1945-1999

92 2000-

After adding the period division, the ss may be added with only one zero. Detailed instructions have been provided to give step by step guidance. A period division is further extendable by the standard subdivisions as taken from 1001-1009 (T3B). Here the ss begins only with a single zero, as per the rule. If needed these ss, especially 08 and 09, may further be extended by the viewpoint Table 3C. For example:

Collection of Victorian Poetry. (English Poetry of the late nineteenth century):

Base (English language literature)	82
Poetry (Form, Table 3B)	1
Victorian period (v.3: 777)	8
Collection (as Instructed under 11-19 Table 3B)	08

Hence the complete class number is

821.808

Similarly:

Critical appraisal of Victorian fiction

82 Base Number

+3 (T3B, Fiction of Specific Period)

+8 (Victorian Period, from Vol. 3 : 777)

+ 0 (As under - 31 - 39, T3B)

+ 9 (As under - 1 - 8 T3B, p. 627, Vol. 1)

=823.809

Social themes in Victorian Fiction

For critical appraisal of Victorian fiction, we have 823.809. Since 08 and 09 are further extendable by Table 3C, we can add to the result the appropriate notation for social themes from Table 3C which is 355. Hence the complete class number is

823.809+355=823.809355

Critical study of plots in post-war American novels:

81 (Base) +3 (Form) +54 (Period) + 0

+ 9(Critical appreciation, Table 3B)

+24 (Plot, Table 3C)

=81+3+54+0+9+24=813.540924

More examples will help to clarify further :

American literature

810

Dictionary of American literature

81+03(ss-03 from T3B)=810.3*

(Note that the base for American literature is 81)

International Conference on American literature

81+0601(ss-0601 from T3B)=810.601*

All India Conference on American Literature

81+060(T1-0603-0609)+54(T2)=810.6054

(We have added-54 from Table 2 to the base number 060 from Table 1. This has been done as per instructions under ss-0603-0609)

History of American literature of the Colonial period

81+0900(T3B)+1=810.9001

Here 1 has been added from the period table for

American literature given at v3:774

History of 20th century American literature

81+0900+5=810.9005

---

* These standard subdivision though used through T_3B are the same as in T_1.

History of American literature for children

81+09(T3B)+9282 notation for children in Table 3C

=81+09+9282=810.99282

History of realism in American literature

81+09+12 (Table 3C realism)=81+09+12=810.912

American poetry

81+1=811

Dictionary of American poetry

81+1003(T3B)=811.003

All India Conference on American Poetry

81+1006(T3B)+0+54(T2)=81+1006054=811.006054

History of American poetry

81+1009 (T3B)=811.009

American epic poetry

81+1032(T3B, p. 628, vol.l)=811.032

Dictionary of American epic poetry

81+1032+03 Dictionary as per instinctions under T3B-102 -107 (p. 628 vol.1)=811.03203

All India Conference on American Epic Poetry

81+1032+06054=811.03206054

History of American epic poetry

81+1032+09=811.03209

Realism in American epic poetry of 20th century: A critical appraisal

Base, American Literature	=	81
Epic poetry (Table 3B)	=	1032
Critical apprisal (from T3B-102-107)	=	09
Period Table 3C (from 01-09)	=	0
20th century (from special Table at 774 p. vol. 3)	=	5
		811.0320905

It may be noted here the "Realism" Facet had to be ignored to accommodate period facet for 20th century.

If we include realism then the period facet i.e. 20th century will have to be ignored :

Base	81
Epic poetry	1032(T3B)
Critical study	09(from - 102-107 under T3B)
Realism	-12 (from T3C)
	= 811.0320912*

Classification of literary works without language or form

Collections from 20th century literature

808.8	Collection from more than two literatures
808.8001-.8005	Collection from specific periods

As per instructions, we are to add to the base number 808.800 the number following 090 in ss notation 0901-0905 from Table 1 = 808.800+4 =808.8004.

(The reader is again reminded here that the period has been taken from the general period table, viz, Table 1.)

Collection of literature on social themes

Collection displaying specific features.

808.801-.803

Here, we are to add to the base number 808.80 notation 1-3 from Table 3C. In Table 3C the notation for social themes is 355. Hence the required class number is

808.80+355(T3C)=808.80355

Collection of epic poetry

(No language and period)

808.81	Collection of poetry
808.812-.817	Collection of specific kinds of poetry

* In case of the choice between the two alternative numbers the later should be preferred.

As per instructions here (p. 768, vol. 3) we are to add to the base number 808.81 the numbers following 10 in 102-107 of Table 3B. The notation for epic poetry is 103. So, as per instructions we are to add 3 to the base 808.81

808.81+3=808.813

Use of Table 3 C

Critical appraisal of Romanticism in 19th century English poetry

82+1+8+09+145=821.809145

Base: English literature	= 82
Poetry (of specific period) -11-19, T3B	= 1
19th century as under 82 (Schedules vol. 3, p. 777)	= 8
Facet indicator as instructed	= 0
(under-11-19 T3B Vol. 1, p. 629)	
Criticism as under -1-8 T3B (p. 627 vol.1)	= 9
Romanticism (T3C)	= 145
	821.809145

Portrayals of children in Victorian English fiction (Period is later 19th century: the Victorian period)

82+3+8+0+9+352(T3C)+3(from 083, Table 1)

= 823.8093523

Accounts of London in English drama of the Queen Anne Period

822+5+0+9+32 (Place from Table 3C) = 822.50932 + specific place from area table = 822.50932 + 421 (Table 2) = 822.50932421

Depiction of India in Victorian fiction

823+8+09+32+54 (Table 2)=823.8093254

Collection of English literature written by Europeans

82+08(T3B)+0+8(From Table 3C)+09(Table 5)=820.80809

Contemporary French literature — a critical appraisal

84+0900(T3B)+914 (For later 20th Century) =840.900914

Romanticism in English poetry

82+100(from - 1001-1009, T3B) + 9 (from-1-8(T3B) + 145(T3C) = 821.009145

Plot in 17th century Spanish novels

86+3+3(Period) + 0 + 9 +24(Table 3C)=863.30924

Description of women in 20th Century English novels

82+3+91(20th century)+0 + 9 +352 (Table 3C) + 2(from 082, Table 1) = 823.91093522

Collection of German language literature written by Englishmen

83+080(Table 3B)+8(Table 3C)+21 (Table 5)=830.80821

Collection of German language literature by Jews

83+080+(T3B)+8+924 (Table 5)=830.808924

Depiction of Indian religions in English literature

82+09(T3B, 091-099)+4(Table 3C)+294 (from the Schedules 001-999) = 820.94294

A critical study of plots in Hindi novels of the early 20th century

891.43	Hindi Literature
3	Fiction (T3B)
6	Period under 891.4 (vol. 3, p 807)
0	as under - 31-39 (T3B, vol. 1, p. 633)
9	from 91-99 under - 1-8 of T3B, vol. 1, p. 627
24	For plot in T3C
	= 891.43360924

Contributions to Hindi literature by Bengalis – a critical study (no form, no period))

891.43+09 (from 091-099 in Table 3B)

+8 (literature for and by various specific ethnic, national groups from Table 3C)

As per instructions, 8 is to be further subdivided by Table 5, where the notation for Bengali people is 9144

Hence the complete number is

891.43098+9144 (Table 5)=891.430989144

Contributions of Bengalis to Hindi poetry (no period)

891.43 + 1009(T3B)+8(T3C)+9144(T5)

=891.43100989144

The contribution of Bengalis to Hindi poetry of the post 1940 era

891.43+1+7 (Period)+0+9 (as under -1-8 T3B)+Table 3C+Table 5

=891.43+1+7 (Period)+09 (ss)+8 (by various national, ethnic groups, Table 3C) +9144 (for Bengalis from Table 5)

=891.43170989144

Depiction of Hinduism in British fiction

82+300 (from -3001-3009 T3B) +9 (from 91-99 of -1-8 (T3B)) + 382 (T3C) + 945 (from 294.5 Hinduism) = 823.009382945

Hinduism in 20th century British fiction

Base: English literature	=	82
Fiction (of specific period) (T3B)	=	3
20th Century as under 820	=	9
Facet indicator as under-31-39 (T3B)	=	0
Description as under	=	9

91-99 of -1-8 T3B, p. 627 vol. I)

Religious themes (Table 3C)	=	382
Hinduism from 294.5	=	945
		823.909382945

Collection of Hindi literature for children

891.43+080 (from 080001-08099 of Table 3B)+9282 (Table 3C)

=891.430809282

Collection of Hindi poetry for children

891.43+100(from-1001-1009 of T3B) + 80 (from 800-809 under - 1-8 of T3B) + 9282 (T3C)

= 891.43100809282

Collection of Modern Hindi poetry for children

891.43+1+7 (Period)+080+(Table 3C)+9282

=891.43170809282

A critical study of women novelists of the Victorian period

82+3(T3B)+8(Victorian Period) + 0 + 9 (from 91-99 under - 1 - 8 of T3B) + 9283 (Women, T3C)

= 823.8099283

The reader may be again reminded that the elements from Table 3 can only be added when instructed to do so in the Schedules. Where a number admits notation from Table 3, such a number is marked with an asterisk. Where there is no asterisk, the number cannot be extended further.

For example,

Chattisgarhi (Hindi) literature

891.49

If we have Chattisgarhi poetry, the class number is still

891.49

Anthology of Kashmiri literature

891.499

Anthology of Bagheli poetry

891.49

(Here no other facet is admissible)

Let us take some more examples:

Stream of Consciousness in 20th century English novels

82+3+9+0+9+25=823.90925

Anthology of French poems composed by Indians

(Here there is no period division)

Base number for French literature 84

Collection of Poetry 100+80

For Indians, as per instruction, the number is to be taken from 93-99 of Table 3C. Here 9 is the base to be further synthesized by Table 2, thus, the number for Indians is

- 9+54=954

Making 10080 as the base, we add to it the number for Indians:

84+1008+0+954=841.0080954

Collection of Hindi lyrical love poetry

891.43+103+08+354=891.4310308354

Critical appraisal of Punjabi satirical poetry by writers living in Canada

891.42	Punjabi literature
107	(T3B)
09	(from - 102 - 107 under T3B, vol. 1, p. 628)
9	(from 93-99 in T3C, p. 650, vol. 1)
71	(Canada, T2)
	= 891.4210709971

Collection of English literature written by children

Base = 82

Collection =080 (Table 3B)

Here we have the instructions to go to Table 3C where number of children writers is 9282:

82+080+9282=820.809282

Critical Appraisal of Hindi short stories written by Punjabis

Base number for Hindi Fiction 891.43

Short Stories 301

Finding instructions, we go to the instructions under Specific forms page vl:628 (T3B)

Critical appraisal 09

Literature for and by various specific racial ethnic national groups 8

8 is further extended by notations 03-99 from Table 5, where the number for Punjabis is 9142

Hence the complete number is

891.43+301+09+8+9142=891.433010989142

A critical appraisal of the poetry of Rabindranath Tagore

891.44+1+5 (Period) =891.4415

Use of Table 3C outside the Main Class 800

Comedy motion pictures

791.4361+7 (from 17 T3C) = 791.43617

Comedy TV programmes

791.4561+7(from 17, T3C) =791.45617

8

Use of Table 4: Subdivisions of Individual Languages and Language Families for the Languages Schedule (400)

This, one of the simplest tables to use, is exclusively used for the Main Class 400 Languages. If need be, it may be extended by the Table 6 Languages. Table 4 lists linguistic problems and elements.

Main Class digit 4 and the language number taken together form the base. The base numbers for all the major languages have been enumerated in the schedules. The base number is further extendable by Table 4 and, if further need be, by Table 6. The facet formula that emerges is:

Base number + Table 4+Table 6

Whenever Table 4 or Table 6 is to be used, sufficient instructions guide us at 410-490 by marking the base number with an asterisk:

Grammar of English Language

Base number for English = 42

Grammar (Table 4) = 5 = 425

(As instructed under 420-490, p. 896, vol. 2)

A study of words of the Sanskrit language

Base number for Sanskrit 491.2

Words (Table 4) 81

491.281

Hindi primer (reader) for semi literates

491.43+862(T_4) = 491.43862

Hindi primer for English speaking learners

491.43+864(T_4)+21 English (T_6) = 491.4386421

English primer for Hindi speaking readers

42+864(T_4)+9143(T_6) = 428.649143

Bilingual Dictionaries

The DDC is able to provide precise class numbers for bilingual dictionaries. Here the language in which the words are given make the base number; to the base from 420-490 is added the digit-3 (from Table 4), which means dictionaries, to the result is added the language number for the language in which meanings are given as taken from Table 6. Thus the formula is:

Base number+3 (Table 4) +second language (Table 6)

For example, take *Sanskrit-German Dictionary*. Here Sanskrit forms the base number, as the entry words are given in Sanskrit.

491.2+3+the number for German from Table 6

=491.2+3+31=491.2331

Similarly, the class number for a

German-Sanskrit dictionary will be

43+3+912=433.912

(Here 43 is the base number for German and 912 the number for Sanskrit as taken from Table 6.)

Similarly:

Russian-Punjabi dictionary

491.7+3+9142=491.739142

English-French Dictionary

42+3+41=423.41

Table 4 may also be supplemented by Table 6 as already shown.

Use of English words in Hindi language.

It is a study of Hindi, so it will form the base number. For foreign elements we have 24 in Table 4 which is further extendable by Table 6:

491.43+24+the number for English from Table 6

=491. 43+24(T4)+21(T6)=491. 432421

Similarly,

French phrases in the English language

42+24+41=422.441

It may further be noted that in the schedule of Main Class 400 Languages class numbers for all the known languages do not exist. But the base number for such unenumerated languages can be crystallised through the use of Table 6. Instructions to add from Table 6 exist in such cases. For example:

Tocharian Language

The class number for it has not been given specifically.

At 491.9, we have Baltic and other languages. Some languages have been enumerated; 491.99 is for other languages. Instructions say that to obtain the class number for other languages, we are to add to 491.99 the number following 9199 in 91991-91998 from Table 6. The number in Table 6 for Tocharian is 91994.

Thus the number for Tocharian is:

491.99+4=491.994

Similarly, let us have the number for Egyptian (It belongs to the family of Hematic and Chad languages whose class number is 493). As per instructions at 493, the class number for Egyptian is:

493+1(from931 (T_6))=493.1

Similarly for Mongolic languages (which belong to the Ural-Altaic languages family (from 9423 (T6)) the base number is 494. The class number thus is:

494+23(from 9423(T6))=494.23

Some other class numbers illustrating the use of Main Class 400:

American English

427.9+73(T2)=427.973

Indian English

427.9+54(T2)=427.954

Pakistani English

427.95491

(In the above two examples, 427.9 has been subdivided by the area table.)

English slang

427.09

English dialect of London

427+1 (from 421 London T_2) = 427.1

West Sussex dialect of English

427+26 (from 4226, T_2)

= 427.26

9

*Use of Table 5 : Ethnic and National Groups**

This table enumerates people based upon their, ethnic, or national origins. In the 18th edition, the use of this table was very limited as it could be used only on invitation, but since the 19th edition, its application has been universalized through the ss 089. It means that a subject can be treated with respect to groups of people characterized by their national, or ethnic origin, even if there are no instructions in the schedules to add from Table 5. Its use is simple: where there are instructions in the Schedules, we are simply to add the notation from Table 5 to the designated base number.

Psychology of the Dutch ethnic groups.

For the psychology of specific ethnic groups, we have the class number

155.84

Under this class number, we have instructions that to the base number 155.84 add the number from Table 5, where

---

* In the previous editions it was named as "Racial, Ethnic and National Grups".

the number for the Dutch is 3931. The full class number therefore is :

155.84+3931 + 155.843931

Similarly, psychology of Danish ethnic groups

155.84+3981=155.843981

Class numbers for some of the lesser known religions are obtainable with the application of Table 5:

299 Religions of other origin

299.92 Religions of other ethnic origins (vol. 2, p. 311)

Here we are instructed to add to the above base the number following 99 in 991-999 from Table 5

Religion of Polynesians

299.92 + 4 (from - 994 T_5) = 299.924

Religion of Khmer people (a religion founded in Southeast Asia)

299.5 + 93 (from 95275) = 299.593

Druidism (a religion of the Celts)

299+16=299.16

Another officially invited use occurs at 305.8 Ethnic and national social groups:

A social study of Bengalis

(Bengalis are a linguistic-ethnic group)

305.8 is the base number to which the notation for Bengalis is to be added from Table 5 as per instructions:

305.8+9144=305.89144

Sociology of Bengali Women

305.4 not 305.89144

305.4 has been preferred over 305.8 as per the preference table as given under 305 (vol. 2, p. 327)

Jewish society

305.8+924=305.8924

Another inevitable use of Table 5 occurs at 641.592 Ethnic cooking. Here instructions exist to add to the above base the notation from Table 5 for the cookery of ethnic groups.

Punjabi cooking

641.592+9142=641.5929142

Punjabi-Canadian Cooking

641.5929142071

Kashmiri cooking

641.592+91499 (T5) = 641.59291499

Another official use of Table 5 is made at 789.21-.29 Music of ethnic and cultural groups. (In DDC22 the class 789 is optional)

Folk music of Punjabis

789.2 + 9142 = 789.29142

Folk music of Pashtuns

789.2+91593=789.291593

Folk music of the Dutch

789.2+3931=789.23931

As per special subdivisions under 789.21-.29 (v3:708) the number extended by Table 5 can be further specified

History of Folk music of Punjabis

789.29142+009=789.29142009

General principles of folk music of Punjabis

789.29142+01 =789.2914201

Instruments of Punjabi folk music

789.29142+02=789.2914202

Flute in Punjabi folk music

789.29142+02+83 (from 788.3)

= 789.291420283

Punjabi folk music in England

789.29142+0+42 (Table 2)

= 789.29142042

Some of the numbers in Table 5 are further divisible by Table 2. For example, in Table 5 the subdivision -68 Spanish Americans is further divisible by national groups of Spanish American by the addition of notation 7-8 from Table 2 to the base number -68.

Colombian people 68+861(T2) = -68861

Bolivians

68+84(T2) = -6884

Therefore, the class number for folk music of Bolivians is:

789.2+6884=789.26884

Similarly, national groups of Arabs are obtainable by the addition of area notation 5-6 from Table 2 to the base number-927(T5).

Libyans

927(T5)+612(T2) = -927612(T5)

Therefore, the class number for Libyan society is:

305.8+927612=305.8927612

Occasionally the area from Table 2 is added through the addition of zero as a facet indicator e.g. -96073 United States Blacks. For US Blacks in Canada the notation may be obtained by adding the area number for Canada to the above base, but through the addition of a zero, (see instructions in Table 5), e.g.:

-96073071

Indians in the US

-91411073

Bengalis in England

-9144+0+42(T2) = -9144042

Brazilians in the USA

-698+0+73(T2) = -698073

Nepalis in India

-91495+0+54(T2) = -91495054

Let us use the above synthesized numbers into full class numbers:

Social study of Indians in the United States.

Here Indians are a national group.

The base class number is 305.8. As per instruction, to this base the number for Indians is added from Table 5.

Social study of Indians

305.8 as given under 305.805-.89 – 91411

= 305.891411

For "Indians in the USA" to the resultant class number add 0 and then the area number for the USA as taken from Table 2.

305.891411+0+73 (Table 2)=305.891411073

Similarly:

Social study of Nepalis in India

305.8+91495054=305.891495054

Folk music of Libyans

789.2+927612 (Table 5) =789.2927612

History of Jews throughout the world

909.04+924 (From Table 5)=909.04924

Similarly:

History of Punjabis in the world

909.04+9142=909.049142

Period subdivisions of **world history** as given under 909.1-909.8 can also be added with a zero as facet indicator.

World history of Punjabis in the 19th century.

909.04+9142 (Table 5)+0+81=909.049142081

World history of Celts in the 20th century

909.04+916 (Table 5)+0+82=909.04916082

Collected biographies of Jews

920.0092+924 (Table 5) = 920.0092924

Collected biographies of Punjabis

920.0092+9142 (Table 5)=920.00929142

Collected biographies of Celts

920.0092+916 (Table 5)=920.0092916

Education of Punjabis in Canada

Education of specific kinds of students 371.82

Students by nationality 9

(As per instruction we have to add to 371.82 the number following-08 in 081-089 (Table 1). There the number for Ethnic groups is 9.)

Punjabis (as-089(T1)) 9142(T5)

is further divisible by T5

in Canada as per instruction in T5 0+71

371.8299142071

Education of Eskimos in the USA

371.829+971 (Table 5)+073=371.829971073

Sinhalese migrant labour in New York State

331.63+9148 (Table 5)+0+747 (Table 2)

=331.6391480747

Use of Table 5 through the standard subdivision - 089

Apart from a few officially recognised situations demanding the use of Table 5, this table can be used anywhere through the use of ss 089:

Child labour among Indians

331.31+089 (Table 1)+91411 (Table 5)

=331.3108991411

Papier-mache among Kashmiris in England

745.542+089+91499+0+42=745.54208991499042

Reading habits of Indians

028.9+089+91411=028.908991411

Reading habits of Indians in England

028.908991411 +0+42=028.908991411042

10

Use of Table 6: Languages

Whenever any subject is further divisible by a language facet, notation from Table 6 is added to the specified base number. Provision of a separate table listing almost all languages has made possible the detailed enumeration of many lesser known languages not hitherto easy to identify.

Table 6 is to be used to supplement any number from the Schedules or even from the Tables (only on invitation). For example, the division of general encyclopaedias has been on broad language groups, which further can be sorted into individual languages by the use of Table 6 :

036 Encyclopaedias in Spanish and Portuguese

For any specific language encyclopaedia in this language group, one has to add to 03 the number for the particular language in 61-69 in Table 6, as per instructions:

Spanish encyclopaedias

036+1(from 61, T_6) = 036.1

Papiamento encyclopaedias

036+8(from 68 T_6) = 036.8

Similarly, 039 is encyclopaedias in other languages (not provided for in 031-038). Class numbers for other encyclopaedias in other languages are to be obtained by adding language notation 7-9 from Table 6 to base number 039.

Vishv Kosh (Encyclopaedia in Hindi)

039+9143(T_6)=039.9143

General encyclopaedias in Japanese

039+956=039.956

Similarly, class numbers for various translations of the Bible are also got by the use of Table 6:

220.5 Modern versions and translations [of the Bible]

220.53-.59 in other languages.

For languages other than English we are asked to add the number for the corresponding language from Table 6 to the specified base 220.5:

The Bible in Hindi

220.5+9143 = 220.59143

The Bible in German

220.5+31=220.531

Vedic literature in English

294.5921+045 (as under 294.592 v2:269) + 21 (T6 as under 045)

= 294.592104521

Though Table 6 has been used at a fairly large number of places in the Schedules, main Classes 400 Languages and 800 Literature appear to be the home fields of its applications. In these two fields, the use of this table has already been discussed and illustrated while dealing with the use of Tables 3 and Table 4 respectively.

In Main Class 400 Languages (vol. 2) all the major languages have been enumerated with the exception of some lesser known languages. But Table 6 contains an almost exhaustive list of all known languages. Therefore, class numbers for these unenumerated languages can be obtained by the use of Table 6 on instructions.

For example:

470 Italic Languages

479 Other Italic Languages

to be obtained by adding to the base number 479 the number following 79 in 794-799 in Table 6.

Study of Faliscan language

Faliscan language is one of the Italic languages, which has not been enumerated under 470-478. Therefore, it will obviously go to 479. In Table 6 under 79 and its parts, we see that the notation for Faliscan is 794. Following the instructions, the class number for Faliscan is:

479+4 (from 794 of Table 6)=479.4

(We have added to 479 the digits following 79, which is 4).

Similar instructions appear at 491.99, 493, 494, 495.92-.97, 496.33,496.391-.399,497,498 and 499.

Again, take the Tupi language (a South American native language). Its class number is:

498+3829 [from 983829(T_6)] = 498.3829

As per instructions notation from T4 can be added to the thus arrived number. For example

Grammar of Tupi

498+3829+5(T4) = 498.38295

Tupi English dictionary

498.3829+3(T4)+21(T6) = 498.3829321

The use of Table 6 in conjunction with Table 4 for bilingual dictionaries in 400 has already been demonstrated in the chapter on the use of Table 4.

In the 800 Literature schedule some of the languages not enumerated can be obtained by the use of Table 6. The use here is similar to its use in 400 languages.

For example, 893 Non-Semitic Afro-Asiatic literature

(Here the particular literature in this family of languages is to be obtained by adding to the base number 893 the numbers following 93 in 931-937 from Table 6.)

Egyptian literature

893+1(from931(T6))=893.1*

(Since 931 is Egyptian in Table 6.)

Similarly:

Somali literature

893+54(from 9354(T_6)) = 893.54*

(The notation for Somali is 9354 in Table 6.)

Another use of Table 6 is at 372.65

Foreign languages in elementary schools.

The teaching of specific foreign languages in elementary schools is got by adding to the base 372.65 the relevant notation 2-9 from Table 6.

Hindi as a second language in elementary schools

372.65+9143(T_6)=372.659143

German as a foreign language in elementary schools

372.65+31(T_6)=372.6531

Class numbers derived from 372.65 can further be synthesised by adding facets enumerated under 372.3-372.8. (p. 800, vol.2)

Curriculums in German as a second language in elementary schools

372.6531+043=372.6531043

Methods for Teaching German as a second language in elementary schools

372.6531+044=372.6531044

Method of teaching English as second language in Primary Schools of India

---

* These numbers can be further extended by Table 3.

372.65+21(T_6)+044 (from 372.6 - 372.8 (vol. 2: 800) + 09 (T_1) + 54 (T_2)

= 372.65210440954

Some more examples:

A general periodical in Hindi

059+9143=059.9143

A general periodical in Romanian

055+91(from 591(T_6))=055.91

A general periodical in Spanish

056+l(from61 (T6))=056.1

A French encyclopaedia

034+1 (from 41 (T_6)) = 034.1

English proverbs

398.9+21=398.921

Spanish proverbs

398.9+61=398.961

Hindi proverbs

398.9+9143=398.99143

Sanskrit calligraphy

745.6199+12 (from 912 (T6)) = 745.619912

English-French dictionary

42+3(Table 4) + 41 (Table 6) = 423.41

For more examples go back to the use of Table 4, Chapter 8.

11

Groups of Persons

This chapter deals with classification of subjects involving persons by their social, psychological, or other individual characteristics, such as health, age, marital status, and profession. This is done through the use of the ss-08 in Table 1 or by making use of the add to ... instruction from the schedules mostly through 011 - 999. For example, take

Baptists as Social Groups.

It is a subject of sociology, where social groups are placed at 305, and here the social stratification of various religious groups is placed under 305.6. Here as per instructions, we are to add to the base 305.6 the number following 2 in 230-290 in the Schedules. The notation for Baptists is 286, so we will add 86 to the designated base:

305.6+86=305.686

is the appropriate class number.

Another such invitation is extended at 390.4 Customs of people by occupations. It is to be further subdivided by 001-999. For example :

Social customs of artists

390.4+7(from 700)=390.47

Customs of lawyers

390.4+34(from 340)=390.434

Similarly, 704 Special topics in the fine and decorative arts can be studied in respect of persons from 04 to 87 as under 704.04.08.

Child artists

704.08+3(from 083 T_1)=704.083

Art works by scientists

704.08+8(from 088 T1) + 5 (for scientists from 001-999 as interested under 088001-088999 (T1, vol. 1, p. 208) = 704.0885

174 is Economic, professional, occupational ethics. Ethics of some of the professions have been enumerated, e.g.:

174.2 Medical professions

174.3 Legal professions

Ethics for all other professions have been placed at 174.9, and we have been asked to get the individual class number for ethics of rest of the professions by adding notation from 001-999 Schedules. For example:

Ethics of librarianship

174.9+02(from 020 in 001-999)2=174.902

Ethics of historians

174.9+907.20 (as under 907.201.209, vol. 3, p. 832) + 2(table 2) = 174.9907202

In addition to its invited use at various places in the schedules, the use of a subject by specified persons has also been suggested in various auxiliary tables. For instance, in Table 1 (Standard subdivisions) 024 Works for specific types of users is further extendable by 001-999 for works specifying the type of user:

Library classification for philosophers

025.42 is classification. For a subject meant for a specific type of user, we have the ss 024, which as per instructions is further divisible by 001-999. For philosophers we have the notation 100 in the schedules. Thus the complete class number is:

025.42+024(T1)+1 (from 001-999)=025.420241

Philosophy for librarians

100+024 (Table 1) + 020 (from 001-999)

= 100 + 024 + 02 = 102.402

Similarly:

Mathematics for engineers =Mathematics for a specific type of user

510+24=510.24

For engineers, we have notation 620 from the schedules, vol. 3

So the complete class number is

510.24+62=510.2462

In such cases, it is essential to differentiate between a subject by a specific group of persons and for a specific group of users.

In the Area Table, 176 denotes regions where specific Religions predominate. Here 176 has been further divided on the basis of some enumerated religions, while all the other unenumerated religions have been placed at 1762-1769, and we are asked to add to 176 the number following 29 in 292-299 in the schedules.

For example, take "Islamic Regions of the World". As per the above instructions, we will add to the base 176 the number following 29 in 292-299, where the number for Islam is 297. Thus the desired notation for the above area is:

-176+7=-1767

Similarly countries where Buddhism prevails is

-176+43 (from 294.3) = -17643

If, say, our title is "Libraries in Islamic Countries of the World ",

we will proceed as follows

General libraries

027

For geographical treatment, we are to add to 027.0 (as the base) the area notation for the specified region from Table 2. The number for Islamic regions as already worked out is 1767. So, the appropriate class number is:

027.0+1767=027.01767

*Wages in Islamic countries

331. 29+1767=331. 291767

Banking system in Islamic countries

332.1+09(Tl)+1767=332.1091767

Political situation in Buddhist countries

320.9+17643=320.917643

To all the subdivisions of notation 1 in Area Table 2 can be added all the subdivisions 3-9 of the Area Table through the facet indicator 0, as prescribed under -1(T_2)vol. 1, p. 217. "Islamic countries of Europe" will be :

- 176(T2)+7(from 297)+0+4(T_2)= -176704

Similarly:

Buddhist countries of Asia is

-176(T2)+43(from 294.3 of schedule) + 0 +5(T2)

= -1764305

Therefore:

---

* In the DDC22 the term used for wages is compensation.

Libraries in Buddhist countries of Asia, is:

027.0+1764305=027.01764305

Libraries in Islamic countries of Asia

027.0+176(T_2)+7(from 297) + 0 + 5(T_2)

= 027.0176705

Political conditions in Buddhist countries of Asia

320.9+1764305=320.91764305

Persons also occur at Table 3C. In Table 3C, 352 is specific kinds of persons as a subject or theme of literature. As per instructions under-352 (in Table 3C) it is further subdivided by the notation 088 from Table 1. It in turn is further extended by occupational groups 001-999. For example :

Treatment of lawyers in literature

-352(T_3C)+088(T1) + 34 = -35208834

(Here 34 is lawyers from 001-999)

Similarly :

Treatment of police officials in literature

-352+088+3632=-3520883632

Portrayals of grandparents in literature

-352+53 (from 0853, T1) =-35253

Let us transform the above numbers into complete examples:

Collection of English poetry about lawyers

82+10080(T3B)+notation from Table 3C

=82+10080+35208834=821.008035208834

Depiction of police officials in English drama

82+200(T_3B)+9+352(T_3C)+088(T_1)+363.2 (from 001-999)

= 822.0093520883632

Portrayal of grandparents in English literature

82+080+35253

=820.8035253

Another use of persons in Table 3C occurs at 92 Literature for and by persons of specific classes. As per instruction at 92 in T3C; we are to add to -9205 – 9207 from T1 or to - 921 any number 001-999 from schedules

Collection of recent Urdu poetry by mathematicians.

Urdu Literature	891 .439
poetry	1
modern period	71
(71 being taken from the period table at 891.4)	
collections, Table 3B	0 +80 (from -1-8 in T_3B)
by specific kinds of persons (Table 3C)	921
by mathematicians from 001-999	51

891.439+1+71+0+80+921+51

=891.43917108092151

Similarly:

Critical appraisal of Hindi poetry composed by physically disabled poets (no period)

891.43+100(T3B, vol. 1, p. 627) +9(from - 1 - 8 in T3B) + 352 (T3C) + 7 (From 087, T1)

= 891.4310093527

Critical appraisal of late 20th century Hindi drama written by blind dramatists

891.43+2+71(period)+0+9(from T_3 B)+352(T_3C) + 71(from 087 in T1)

=891.432710935271

(Here

2 drama from Table 3

71 is period from another special period table (v3:807)

0 as given under -1-2 (T_3B)

9 critical appraisal from Table 3B

352 literature by special kind of person from Table 3C

71 (from 0871 in T_1)

Collection of recent Urdu poetry composed by Hindus

891.439+1(T_3B)+72 (Period from (891.4) + 0 + 80 (as under -1-8 T_3B) + 352(T_3C) + 8 (from 088T_1) + 2945 (from 001-999 Schedules)

= 891.43917208035282945

Collection of English poetry composed by professional historians (no specific period)

82+100(from - 1001 - 109, T3B, Vol. 1, p. 627) + 921 (T3C) + 907.20 (under 907.201 - .209, vol 3, p. 832) + 2 (T2)

= 821.00921907202

Art works by scientists

704.08+8(from 088, T1) + 5 (for scientists from 001-999 as instructed under 088001-088999(T1, vol. 1, p 208)

= 704.0885

12

Examples Illustrating Multiple Synthesis

Multiple synthesis is defined as number building process by adding notations, to a given base number, taken from more than one place.

Liver diseases

616.362

Microbiology of liver diseases

616.362+01=616.36201

Bacterial diseases of the liver

616.362+01+4=616.362014

(Added to 01 the number following

616.01 in 616.014-616.019;

the number for bacteria is 014,

hence 4 has been added)

Similarly,

Spirochaetales in liver diseases in human beings (a kind of bacterial disease of the liver).

Bacterial diseases of the liver is:

616.362+014

To the base of 616.014 we are to add the number following 589.9 in 589.92 - 589.99 where Spirochaetales is 589.99 so we are to add 9 only:

616.362+01+4+9=616.3620149

Domestic dogs

636.7

Veterinary medicine for domestic dogs

It will fall under

636.7001–636.708 (p. 345 vol 3)

As per instructions, we are to add to the base 636.70 the numbers following 636.0 in 636.001-636.08. There veterinary medicine is 636.089. So, we will add to 636.70 the number following :

636.0, i.e., 89

Hence the number is:

636.70+89=636.7089

Dog anatomy

Domestic animal anatomy is a subject of veterinary medicine, so we will first reach the above number as before:

636.7089

To arrive at the number for anatomy of the dog, we will add to 636.089 the number following 61 in 610-619: where anatomy is 611, thus we will add 1.

Dog anatomy is

636.7089+1 (from 611 as instructed under 636.089)

= 636.70891

The anatomy of the lungs of dogs

636.7089+124(from 611.24)=636.7089124

Encyclopaedia of the anatomy of the dog

636.7089+1003(from 611.003)=636.70891003

Note that the class number for an encyclopaedia of anatomy is

611.003.

Tissue biology of dogs

636.7089+10189(from611.0189)=636.708910189

Anatomy of the tooth tissue of dogs

First we will build the class number for the anatomy of dog tissues

636.7089+10189=636.708910189

There at 611.0189, to build the class number for tooth tissue, we have to add to 611.0189 the element for tooth tissue to be taken from 611.1-611.9, where the number for tooth is 611.314.

Thus, the class number for tooth tissue is

611.0189+314=611.0189314

Anatomy of tooth tissues of dogs

636.708910189+314=636.708910189314

Blood cancer in dogs

Dogs in animal husbandry 636.7

General principles of the animal husbandry of dogs has been placed at

636.7001-.708

Veterinary medicine of dogs

636.70+89=636.7089

For specific aspects of veterninary medicine, we will add to 089, the numbers following 61 in 610-619 where blood cancer is 616.99418. Hence, we will add the number following 61, viz., 699418 to the above number. Hence,

636.7089+699418=636.7089699418

But if it is the **Bone cancer in dogs,** we will have to synthesize 616.994 by the appropriate division of 611 where bone is 611.71

Hence the complete class number is:

636.7089+6994+71=636.7089699471

To repeat: Bone cancer in dogs

Dogs = 636.7

specific topics in dog husbandry = 636.7001-.708

Base number for dog husbandry = 636.70

Veterinary medicine of dogs = 89 (from 636.089)

Cancer = 6994 (from 616.994)

Bone (organs under 616.9942-.9949) = 71 (from 611.71)

636.7089699471

The following chart will further illustrate:

Animal husbandry	Animal husbandry of horses	Animal husbandry of dogs
636	636.1	636.7
Veterinary medicine	Veterinary medicine of horses	Veterinary medicine of dogs
636.089	636.10+89= 636.1089	636.70+89= 636.7089
Veterinary anatomy	(Veterinary) anatomy of horses	(veterinary) anatomy of dogs
636.089+1= 636.0891	636.1089+1 =636.10891	636.7089+1 =636.70891
Veterinary anatomy of lungs	Anatomy of horses lungs	Anatomy of dog lungs
636.089+124 =636.089124	636.1+089+124 =636.1089124	636.7+089+ 124=636.7089124

Similarly:

Lung cancer in horses

636.1 + 089 + 6994 (from 616.994) + 24 (from 611.24) = 636.1089699424

Intestine cancer in cattle

636.2+089 (from 636.089)+6994(from 616.994)+34(from 611.34) = 636.2089699434

Tuberculosis in cattle

636.2+089+6995=636.20896995

Bone tuberculosis in cattle

636.2+089+6995+71=636.2089699571

X-ray diagnosis of lung tuberculosis in horses

636.1+089+6995+24+07+572

=636.108969952407572

It is explained as below:

636.1	Animal husbandry of horses
0	Facet indicator
89	Veterinary medicine
6995	The number following 61 in 610-619 where number for TB is 616.995
24	Lungs: under 616.995 there is instruction to add to base 616.995, the number following 611 in 611.2-611.9, where class number for lungs is 611.24
07	Pathology; added as instructed under 616.1-616.9 (p. 86.vol. 3)
572	X-ray diagnosis; we are asked to add to 07 the number following 616.07 in 616.071-616.079 where 616.07572 is X-ray diagnosis.

Some more examples of synthesis:

Administration of a science library

Administration of a specific type of library 025.19

(Here, we have been instructed to add to the above base the number following 02 in 026-027, and the number for libraries devoted to a specific subject is 026, hence we will add 6 6

026 is further subdivided like 001-999, and the number for science is 500

Hence the class number is: 025.19+6+5= 025.1965

Similarly:

Administration of special libraries on Indian history

025.19+6+954=025.196954

Administration of public libraries in India

025.19+74(from027.4)+54(T2)=025.197454

Rajya Sabha (Upper House of the Indian parliament)

Legislative bodies have been placed at 328, which is to be subdivided by areas given under 328.4-.9

328+54(T2)=328.54 Indian parliament

Now, as per instructions under 328.4-.9, we are to add the special subdivisions enumerated there; houses of parliament fall under the subdivision 07, which is further to be subdivided like 328.304-328.39, the class number for an upper house is 328.31 Hence, we will add 1 to 07, and then will add this result 071 to 328.54, the complete class number being:

328+54+07+1=328.54071

Similarly:

Financial powers of the US Senate

328.73+07+412(from328.3412)=328.7307412

Again

331.124	Job vacancies [labour economics]
331.1242-.1249	Job vacancies in technological, manufacturing, agricultural, etc. occupations.

We are required to add to 331.124 numbers following 6 in 620-690.

Let us take:

Job opportunities in agriculture

331.124+30=331.1243

(The class number for agriculture is 630.)

Similarly:

Job opportunities in cotton agriculture

331.124+3351=331.1243351

The agriculture of cotton is 633.51, and we have added to the designated base the number following 6 in 633.51, viz, 3351).

Job opportunities in cotton storing

Since 633.51 is further extendable by 631.5, and the class number for cotton storing is

633.51+68=633.5168

Hence the complete class number for job opportunities in Cotton storing is:

331.124+3351+68=331.124335168

International law for trade in specific commodities

343.0871–.0875

For individualizing specific commodities, we are required to add to the base 343.087 the numbers following 381.4 in 381.41-.45.

For trade in agricultural commodities we have 381.41. So we will add 1, viz., the digit following 381.4 to the base number 343.087

343.087 + 1 = 343.0871

Not only this, the various agricultural products can further be individualised by the digits following 63 in 633-638.

International law of trade in wheat

343.087 + 1 +311 = 343.0871311

(As the class number for wheat is 633.11 and we have added the digits following 63 in 633-638.)

Similarly:

International law of trade in coffee

343.087+1 (from 381.41) +373 (from 633.73 coffee) = 343.0871373

Public administration in Communist countries

351.1 + 717 (from 1717 (T_2)) = 351.1717

Public administration in India

351 + 54(T_2) = 351.54

Public administration in India : An encyclopedia

351+54(T2)+003(T1)=351.54003

Ministry of Finance of the Government of India

352.4 + 09 (Tl) + 54 (T2) = 352.40954

President of the Republic of India

352.333 + 09 (as under 352-354) + 54 (T2) = 352.3330954

State administration in India

352.13 + 09 (as under 352.13 - 352.19) + 54 (T2) = 352.130954

Panchayati Raj system in India

352.17 + 09 (as under 352.13-352 19) + 54 (T2) = 352.170954

Civil service system in India

352.63 + 09 (as under 352-354) + 54 (T2) = 352.630954

As option A under 093-099 of 352.354 *(p. 625, vol.2)*, the alternative number is:

351 + 54(T2) + 0 (as under 02-04 of 351.3-9) + 263 (from 352.63) = 351.540263

Encyclopedia on the administration of justice

353.4 + 03(T1) = 353.403

Administration of justice in India

353.4 + 09 (as under 352-354) + 54 (T2) = 353.40954

As Option A

351 + 54 (T2) + 0 (as under 02-04 of 351.3-.9) + 34 (from 353.4) = 351.54034

Systems for civil services examination in Indian States

362.65 + 21 (as under 352-354) + 3 (from 352.13 state administration) + 0954 (as under 352.13) = 362.652130954

Revenue administration in India

352.44 + 09 + 54 (T2) = 352.440954

or

351 + 54 (T2) + 0 + 244 (from 352.44) = 351.540244

Proposed budget of the Government of India

352.4 + 54 (T2) (as instructed under 352.493 - .499) + 01 (as under 352.493 - .499) = 352.45401

Agriculture budget of India

354.5 + 2 (as under 22-26 under 352 - 354) + 49 (from 352.49, as instructed under 352.493-.499) + 54 (T2 as instructed above) + 01 (special subdivision as under 352.493 - .499) = 354.52495401

Budget for social welfare programmes in India

353.5 + 2 (as under 22-26 of 352 - 354 (vol. 2, p. 625)) + 49 (from 352.49 as under 352.433 - .499) = 353.5249

Public administration of the economy in India

354 + 0954 (as under 093 - 099 of 352 - 354)

= 354.0954 or

351 + 54 (T2) as instructed under 351.3 - .9) + 0 (as under 02 - 04) + 4 (from 354) = 351.5404

Ministry of home affairs of the Government of India

353.3 + 0954 (as under 093 - 099 of 352 - 354)

= 353.30954

or

351 + 54 (T2) + 0 + 33 (from 353.3) = 351.54033

Police services administration in Madhya Pradesh

353.36 + 09543 (for Madhya Pradesh)

= 353.3609543

or

351+543 (T2) + 0 + 336 (from 353.36) = 351.5430336

Public administration of the postal services in India

354.759 + 0954 =354.7590954

or

351+54 (T2)+ 0 + 4759 (from 354.759) = 351.5404759

Corruption in India

353.46 + 0954=353.460954

or

351+54 (T2) + 0 + 346 (from 353.46) = 351.540346

Teaching methods for problem students

371.93 + 3 (from 371.9043) = 371.933

Teaching problem students through educational games

371.93 + 3 (from 371.9043) + 37 (from 371.337)

= 371.93337

Curriculum research in India

375.00072054

Curriculum in computer studies at primary level

372.34 + 043 (from under 372.8) = 372.34043

Teaching of English as a second language in primary schools

372.65 + 21 (T6) + 044 (from under 372.3 - 372.8)

= 372.6521044

Educational policy of India

379.54

Management of E-mail

384.34 + 068 (Tl) = 384.34068

Email business companies in India

384.34+065+54(T2) = 384.3406554

Biophysics of mammals

571.4 Biophysics

Here as per asterisked footnote we have been asked to add as instructed under 571 - 572 (p. 1090, vol. 2). Here we are to add to the base 571.4 the number following 571 in 571.01 -571.2. The number for animals is 571.1. Hence we will add 1 to 571.4 i.e. 571.4 + 1 Biophysics of Animals.

571.1 can be further subdivided by the number following 59 in 590.1 - 599. The number for mammals is 599. Hence we will further add 9 to make 571.41 + 9 = 571.419 Biophysics of Mammals.

Similarly, Effects of electricity in mammals

571.47 + 1 (from 571.1) + 9 (from 599 mammals)

= 571.4719

Physiology of mammals

571.1 +9 (from 599) = 571.19

Physiology of primates

571.1 + 98 (from 599.8) = 571.198

Effect of cosmic rays on plants

571.459 + 2 (from 571.2 as under 571 - 572)

= 571.4592

Effect of electricity on cells

571.634+7(from 571.47)= 571.6347

Ecology of the Indian Ocean area

577.7 + 5 (from 165 (T2)) = 577.75

Autoecology of the Indian Ocean area

577.7 + 5 + 0 + 26 (from 577.26 as instructed under 577.73 - .75) = 577.75026

A dictionary of bryophyte

588 + 03 (as instructed under 583 - 588, p 1160) vol. 2) = 588.03

Genetical study of bryophyte

588 + 1 (as under 583 - 588) + 35 (from 581.35) = 588.135

Genetics of worms

592.3 + 1 (as under 592 - 599) + 35 (from 591.35) = 592.3135

Atlas of the monkey brain

573.86 + 1 (Animals from 571.1) + 98 (from 599.8 monkeys) + 028 (Tl, as under 592 - 599) = 573.86198028

Similarly:

Effect of cosmic rays on Dicotyledons

571.459+2(from 571.2 as instructed under 571-572, p. 1090, vol.2)

+3 (Dicotyledons 583, as instructed under 571.201 -.28) =571.459+2+3=571.45923

Effect of cosmic rays on the seeds of the dicotyledons

571.459 + 2 + 3 (Dicotyledons) + 467 (from 581.467 seeds) = 571.45923467

Similarly

Effect of High temperature on Roses

571.467+2+3734 (from 583.734 Roses) =571.46723734

Genetics of Gymnosperms

585+1 (as under 583-588, p. 1160, vol.2) +35(from 581.35 Genetics)=585.135

Evolution of Cryptogamia

586+1+38(from 581.38 Evolution)=586.138

Evolution of insects

595.7+1 (as instructed under 592-599 p. 1186 vol.2)+38 (from 591.38 Evolution)=595.7138

Genetic variation in Mollusca

594.0+15+8=594.0158

(We have added to the base 594.0 the digits following 591 in 591.1-591.8, where the number for Genetics is 591.15. The latter is further divisible.)

Radiogenetics of Mollusca

594.0+15+92=594.01592

That is also true of any specified Mollusca.

Evolution of Cockroaches

595.728+1+38=595.728138

Synthetic organic drugs

615.31

We are asked to add to 615.31 the digits following 547.0 in 547.01-547.08 for specific synthetic drugs of organic nature.

For example:

Organometallic synthetic drugs

615.31+5=615.315

(As the number for organometallic compounds is 547.05, and we have added to the base 615.31 the digit following 547.0, viz., 5.)

This can further be synthesized to arrive at any specific organometallic drug:

For example:

Organosodium synthetic drugs.

For organometallic drugs, we have 615.315, as above, under 547.05, we see that to obtain a class number for any specified organometallic compound, we have to add to 547.05 the digits following 546 in 546.38-546.72, the number for sodium in the above span is 546.382, so we will add 382 to the above worked out number.

615.315+382=615.315382

Similarly:

Organo-nickel synthetic drugs

615.31+5+625=615.315625

(The class number for nickel is 546.625.)

Organo-zinc synthetic drugs

615.31+5+661=615.315661

(The class number for zinc is 546.661.)

Electrotherapy for heart diseases:

For heart diseases, we have

616.12

The asterisk here leads us to the special subdivisions under 616.1-616.9 (on pages v. 3: 82-86)

As per instructions, for therapy, we add 06.

Thus for therapies for heart diseases we have

616.12+06=616.1206

But for specific therapies we have to add to 06 the digits following 615.8 in 615.82-615.89. Since the number for electrotherapy is 615.845, we will add 45 to the above

616.12+06+45=616.120645 is the complete number.

Similarly:

Electrotherapy for blood diseases

616.15+06+45(from 615.845 Electrotherapy)
=616.150645

X-ray therapy for blood diseases

616.15+06+422 (From 615.8422 x-ray therapy)
=616.1506422

Pathology of female infertility

For female infertility, we have

618.178

The asterisk here leads us to 618.1-618.8, where pathology is 07. Hence, the complete class number is:

618.178+07=618.17807

The subdivision 07 can be further subdivided like 616.07 if the aspect of pathology is specified :

Diagnosis of female infertility

618.178+07+5=618.178075

(We have added to 07 the digits following 616.07 in 606.077-606.079; as the number for diagnosis is 606.075, we have added 5.)

Similarly :

Diagnosis of diseases of pregnancy

618.3+07+5(from 616.075 Diagnosis)=618.3075

Chemical diagnosis of pregnancy diseases

618.3+07+56(from 616.0756 Chemical diagnosis)
= 618.30756

Animal pests of wheat

Here the agriculture of wheat is 633.11. The asterisk leads us to the instructions under 633-635 (v.3:310), and we are required to add 9 to the base number 633.11 for injuries, pests, and diseases. For specific kinds of injuries/diseases/pests, we are asked to divide the resulting number like 632.1-

632.9. The number for animal pests is 632.6; so we will add 6 to the above. Hence,

633.11+9+6(from 632.6 Animal pests)=633.1196

Individual animal pests can be specified as instructed under 632.6. Let us say :

Monkeys as wheat pests

wheat	633.11	
pests	9	(as under 633-635)
animal pests	6	

(We have added the digits following 632 in 632.1-632.9, and for animal pests the number is 632.6.)

Monkey 98

(We have added to 6 the digits following 59 in 592-599, where the number for monkeys is 599.8.)

Hence the complete class number is

633.11 +9+6+98=633.119698

Similarly:

Rats as wheat pests

633.11+9+6+935=633.1196935

(The class number for rats is 599.35)

Rats as rice pests

633.18+9+6+935=633.1896935

Rats as potato pests

635.21+9+6+935=635.2196935

Insect pests for grapes

Grape growing	634.8
Pests of Grapes	634.82

(We have been asked to add to the base number 634.82 the digits following 632 in 632.1-632.9, where the number for insect pests is 632.7. So, we will add 7, and the complete class number is

634.82+7=634.827

As per instructions under 632.7 we can individualize the various insect pests:

Say our title is:

Beetles as grape pests

Insect pests of grapes 634.82+7

To the above, we are to add the digits following 595.7 in 595.72-595.79. As the number for beetles is 595.76, we will add 6. Hence the complete class number is:

634.82+7+6=634.8276

Similarly:

Locust depradation of grapes

634.82 + 7(from 632.7 insect pests)

+ 26 (from 595.726 Locust)=634.82726

Bees as pests of oranges

634.31 +9+7+99(from 595.799 Bees)=634.319799

Bees as apple pests

634.11+9+7+99=634.119799

Applied physical chemistry (viz., application of physical chemistry in chemical technology).

660.29

For specific aspects of physical chemistry, we are to divide the above number as the base like 541.33-541.39. Let our title be

Applied photochemistry of specific radiations

660.29+53=660.2953

(The class number for photochemistry of specific radiations is 541.353. We have added to the base the digits following 541.3, viz., 53.)

Manufacture of equipment for shooting reptiles

Manufacture of equipment for hunting, fishing, and shooting has been placed at 688.79

We have been asked to divide this class number like 799.1-799.3, and shooting reptiles is 799.279.

Hence the complete class number is

688.79+279=688.79279

As per instructions under 799.279 class numbers for equipment for shooting individual kinds of reptiles can be individualized:

Manufacture of equipment for shooting crocodiles.

For reptiles shooting we have 688.79279. We have been asked at 799.279 to add further the digits following 597.9 in 597.92-597.98. So we will add 8 as the class number for crocodiles is 597.98. Hence

688.79+279+8=688.792798 is the complete class number.

Similarly:

Equipment for shooting turtles (reptiles)

688.79+279(from 799.279 shooting reptiles) + 2(from 597.92 Turtles)=688.792792

(The class number for turtles is 597.92.)

Manufacture of equipment for shooting ducks

688.79+248(from 799.248 shooting water birds)+41 (598.41 Ducks)=688.7924841

(The class number for ducks is 598.41.)

Manufacture of equipment for shooting turkeys

688.79+248+645(from 598.645 Turkeys)

=688.79248645

Flute music

788.32

Techniquès for playing flute

788.32+1 (as under 784-789)+93(from 784.193)

=788.32193

Dance music festivals in India

781.554+079(from 01-09 as instructed under 781.2-781.8)+54(T2) as under 780.79)

=781.55407954

Composition of dance music

781.554+1 +3(from 781.3)=781.55413

Religious principles for the composition of Hindu sacred music

781.7+45 (from 294.5 Hinduism)+0+3312 (from 781.3312)

= 781.74503312

13

Classification of General Statistics, Law, Geography, and History

All these subjects have a common feature that the area though taken from Table 2 is in fact a subject division, and usually occurs as an intervening facet instead of being the last one. It means the area notation is usually further extended by some subject division.

General Statistics 310

The formula for general statistics of specific countries and localities is:

31 (base)+area (from T 2)

General statistics of Asia

31+5(T 2)=315

General statistics of India

31+54(T_2)=315.4

General statistics of Gujarat

31+5475 (T_2)=315.475

Law 340

Law has been first divided by its major branches preceded by international law:

341 Law of nations (International law)

342 Constitutional and administrative law

343 Military, tax, trade and industrial law

344 Labour, social, education and cultural law

345 Criminal law

346 Private law

347 Civil procedure and courts

348 Laws (Statutes), regulations, cases

349 Law of specific jurisdiction and areas

Then in the schedules each branch has been divided by the topic, and each topic under every branch begins with a zero:

344.01 Labour law

344.02 Social insurance law

and so on.

But the preferred arrangement in the DDC is as follows.

The branch is first divided by the jurisdiction and then by the topic of law:

34X+area number+0X (ie. 01-09)

is the citation order:

(Where the first X stands for the branch of the law and the second for the subtopic of the corresponding branch.)

Let us say: Labor law in India:

Labor Law, a division of 344 is 344.01. But as per the above citation order given under 344.3-.9 (p. 585 vol.2), we have

344+54(India from table 2)+01 (topic: labor law)

=344.5401

Obviously this citation order helps tc bring together by country all the subtopics of a branch of law:

Similarly:

Law of public health in India

$344+54(T_2)+04=344.5404$

U.S. public health law

344+73(from 344.04)+04 = 344.7304

Indian Law against abortion

$344+54(T_2)+04194 = 344.5404194$

Indian law for the control of Aids

344+54(T2)+043(from 344.043) + 69792 (from 616.9792 Aids)=344.5404369792

Library legislation in Punjab

344+54552+092=344.54552092

Supreme Court of India

347+54+035=347.54035

As per instructions, this can further be subdivided by some special subdivisions enumerated under 347.02-347.04 (p. 606: vol. 2)

Judges of the Supreme Court of India.

347.54035+34=347.5403534

(34 is for judges as given under

347.02-347.04 p. 606 vol.2)

Court rules of the High court of Rajasthan

347+544(T2)+033(from 347.033)+5(as given under 347.02-347.04)+1(from347.051)=347.54403351

Law of evidence in India

347+54+06=347.5406

Indian marriage Law

346+54+016=346.54016

Marriage law of Texas (USA)

346+764+016=346.764016

Court decisions on the marriage law in India

346+54(T2)+016(from 346.016)+02643(as given under , p. 546-547, vol.2)=346.5401602643

There are also some other topics where subject subdivisions are added after the area. Take for example:

338.93-.99 Economic development and growth in specific continents, countries, localities

Economic policies of the USA

338.973

Economic subsidies in the USA

338.97302

(We have added to the base 338.973, a zero and the digits following 338.92 in 338.922-338.927 where 338.922 is subsidies.)

Similarly:

Nationalization of industry in India

338.9+54(Table 2)+0+4(from 338.924)=338.95404

Communist parties in India

324.2+54(Table 2)+075 (subdivision under

324.24-.29)=324.254075

Conservative political parties in Pakistan

324.2549104

Rules and procedure of the US senate

328+73+05=328.7305

Debates in British Parliament

328+41 (Table 2)+02=328.4102

Financial powers of the Legislative Assembly of Tamil Nadu

328+5482(T2)+07(as under 328.4-.9)+412 (from 328.3412)

= 328.548207412

Geography and History

In the case of geography, the formula is

91+area from T_2+special subdivision (under 913-919, page v3:842+845)

Travels in Mughal India

91+54(Table 2)+04(page v3:842)+25(from 954.025) as instructed under 041-049 (p. 843, vol. 3)

= 915.40425

The geography of coastal regions of India

91+54(Table 2)+09 (page v3:845)+46 (from 146 of Table 2)

=915.40946

General geography of Christian-dominated areas of India

91+54+09+761 (from 1761 of Table 2)=915.409761

General geography of Muslim-dominated areas of Uttar Pradesh.

91+542+09+76 (from 176 of Table 2)+7(from 297 of schedules)=915.4209767

Travels in ancient China

91+31+04(special subdivisions under 914-919)

=913.104

Physical geography of ancient Macedonia

91+381+02=913.8102

Physical geography of the United States

91+73+02=917.302

General geography of the forest regions of Texas

91+764+09 (special subdivision under 913-919) +52(from 152 in Table 2) =917.640952

Geography of the Hilly regions of Greater Punjab of India

91+545+09+43(from 143 T_2)=915.450943

Similarly, the formula for history is:

9+(area from Table 2)+period subdivision from 930-990)

History of India

9+54=954

India under the reign of Akbar

9+54+0254(from 954.0254)=954.0254

History of Punjab

9+545(from Table 2)=954.5

History of Punjab during the reign of Akbar

9+545 (Table 2)+0254(from 954.0254)=954.50254

History of Jammu & Kashmir during British Rule

9+546+03=954.603

History of islands of India

954+009 (from 0091-0098 under 930-990)+42 (from 142 (T2) Islands) = 954.00942

History of Christian regions in India

954+009+761 (from 1761 (T2)) = 954.009761

History of Muslim regions in India

954.009+176(T_2) + 7 (from 297 Schedules) = 954.0091767

14

Exercises for Self Practice

(A) Use of standard subdivision

1. History of World Trade Organisation (WTO)
2. Journal of aptitude tests
3. Research in public administration in the U.K.
4. Chain store organization in Germany
5. Research in algebra
6. Research in algebra in India
7. Research in vocabulary control in the UK
8. Indian trade catalogues of furnitures
9. Directory of universities teaching journalism in Developing Countries
10. Journalism in the 19th century
11. Journalism in the U.K. in the 19th century
12. Journalism in the British colonies in the 19th century
13. Journalism in Muslim countries
14. Journalism in Muslim countries in the 19th century
15. Journalism in Portuguese-speaking areas of India

16. Journalism in Canada in the 19th century
17. Females in the media
18. Women journalists
19. Contributions of Pakistanis to media
20. Economic conditions in Muslim-dominated parts of India
21. Economic conditions in Christian-dominated parts of India
22. Economic conditions in India during 1947-1971
23. Political conditions in Non-aligned countries of Africa
24. Social change in Hindi-speaking areas of India
25. Rural development in India
26. History of the Third World
27. History of the Third World during 1960-1969
28. World history of the Communist bloc
29. History of Christian nations since the 19th century
30. History of English-speaking nations

(B) Titles requiring the addition of two areas from Table 2

31. Migration of people from India to the USA
32. Migration to the USA from poor countries
33. Migration of Buddhists to Europe
34. Exchange rate between the US dollar and the Indian rupee
36. British colonies in Asia
37. British colonies in the Indian Ocean area
38. Artists in Muslim regions of India
39. Muslim artists
40. African American artists
41. British financial investment in the Third World
42. U.S. foreign investment in Pakistan

43. Emigration from India to the U.S.A.
44. Sino- U.S. foreign relations
45. Foreign relations between U.S.A. and the Communist bloc
46. Foreign relations of Israel with Muslim countries
47. Foreign relations of Israel with Muslim countries of Asia
48. Foreign relations of India with British Commonwealth countries
49. Foreign relations of British Commonwealth countries of Asia
50. Labour workers from Nepal in India
51. Labour workers from Pakistan in the Middle East
52. India's economic assistance to Nepal
53. Economic aid from the U.S.A. to developing countries
54. Economic aid from British Commonwealth countries to poor nations
55. Russian economic aid to the Communist bloc in Europe
56. Trade between Japan and Canada
57. Trade between the Communist bloc and the Third World
58. Trade agreements between India and the U.S.A.
59. Trade agreements between Non-aligned nations
60. Public libraries in developing countries
61. Indian educational assistance to Nepal

(C) Illustrations Depicting Synthesis in the Schedules

62. Administration of university libraries
63. Administration of university libraries in India
64. Document selection in university libraries
65. Book selection in prison libraries
66. Book selection on international law

67. Book selection on the history of the U.S. Civil War (1861-1865)
68. Book selection on collection development in libraries
69. Selection and procurement of government publications
70. Acquisition of microforms in libraries
71. Problems of serial procurement in natural science in public libraries
72. Reference service in children libraries
73. Science journalism
74. Sports journalism
75. Aptitude tests for the medical profession
76. Aptitude tests for media
77. Psychology of deaf
78. Emotions and feelings in animals
79. Astronomy as treated in the Bible
80. The Old Testament in Hindi
81. Historical books of the Old Testament in Hindi
82. The Ten Commandments in Hindi
83. The New Testament in Hindi
84. Doctrines of Eastern churches
85. Sacred shrines of Jains
86. The Jains religious calendar
87. Job opportunities in documentation
88. Job opportunities in agriculture
89. Employment market for librarians.
90. Employment opportunities.
91. Compensation and conditions of employment in agricultural occupations
92. Wages of documentationlist
93. Wages in agricultural occupations

94. Trade unions of librarians
95. Agricultural workers union
96. Labour management disputes in documentation centres
97. Labour disputes of agriculture labour
98. Strikes by documentationlists
99. Strikes by agricultural workers
100. Documentation cooperatives
101. Cooperative agriculture
102. Economics of poultry farming
103. Economics of metal extraction
104. Debates in Rashtriya Panchayat (Parliament) of Nepal
105. Social welfare services for cancer patients
106. Social welfare for persons suffering from lung cancer
107. Welfare services for leprosy victims
108. Reform movements for alcoholics
109. Counseling for narcotics addicts
110. Social asylums for the mentally retarded
111. Providing shelter for flood victims
112. Teaching methods for slow learners
113. Teaching equipment for the education of the mentally retarded
114. Corporal punishment in elementary schools
115. Teaching through audio-visuals in elementary schools
116. Science curriculum in elementary schools
117. Corporal punishment in secondary schools
118. Teaching through audio-visuals in secondary schools
119. Teaching through audio-visuals in universities
120. Midday meal to students in elementary schools
121. Folk tales about elephants
122. Folk tales about the intelligence of elephants

123. The rose in folk tales
124. Satellites of the planet Saturn
125. Orbits of the satellites of the planet Saturn
126. Hindu chronological calendar
127. Acceleration of meson particles
128. Radio isotopes of radium
129. Physical chemistry of organic substances
130. Radioactive isotopes of organic substances
131. Radioactive isotopes of hydrocarbons
132. Radioactive isotopes of the aromatic hydrocarbons
133. Analytical biochemistry of plants
134. Biochemistry of cryptogamia
135. Biophysics of cryptogamia
136. Analytical biochemistry of cryptogamia
137. Animal biochemistry
138. Analytical biochemistry of animals
139. Role of sugar in animal biochemistry
140. Function of proteins in animal biochemistry
141. Biochemistry of steroids (organic compounds) in invertebrates
142. Glucose in the biochemistry of insects
143. Biochemistry of Orthoptera
144. Analytical biochemistry of Orthoptera
145. Biochemistry of enzymes in Orthoptera
146. Regional physiology of the human head
147. Organometallic synthetic drugs
148. Synthetic organic drugs of sulfites
149. Synthetic organoaluminum drugs
150. Synthetic organopotassium drugs
151. Copper poisons

152. Lead poisons
153. Diagnosis of lung diseases
154. Electrical diagnosis of lung diseases
155. Spurious therapies of smallpox
156. Electrotherapy for diseases of bones
157. Electrotherapy for Arthritis,
158. Climatotherapy for tuberculosis
159. Climatotherapy for tuberculosis of bones
160. X-ray diagnosis of bone tuberculosis
161. Rib fractures
162. Drug therapy for dental diseases
163. Electrotherapy for diseases of the gums
164. Case histories in children's diseases
165. Lighting in museums
166. Lighting in science museums
167. Lighting in biological museums
168. Lighting in theaters
169. Lighting in hospital libraries
170. Concrete as a foundation material in civil engineering
171. Repair of bicycles
172. Chemistry of agriculture
173. Physical chemistry of agriculture
174. Fertilizers for fruit orchards
175. Nitrate fertilizers for fruit orchards
176. Nitrate fertilizers for citrus fruits
177. Nitrate fertilizers for flower and ornamental plants
178. Poultry feed
179. Snake farming [Snakes are reptiles]
180. Butterfly gardening in Asia

181. Snake farming in South India
182. Cereals foods
183. Home construction of raincoats for women
184. Rearing of problem children
185. Home care for deaf children
186. Upbringing of Jewish children
187. Rearing of Jewish children in the U.S.A.
188. Rearing of Punjabi children in Canada
189. Cost accounting in hospitals
190. Cost accounting in government offices
191. Audit reports of hospital accounts
192. Industrial production of nitrogen compounds
193. Industrial thermochemistry
194. Industrial properties of anthracite coal
195. Pasteurization in the industrial production of wines
196. Journal of pottery technology
197. Research in pottery technology
198. Research in the U.S.A. in pottery technology
199. All-India Conference on pottery Technology
200. Industrial dyeing of silk
201. Industrial dying of polyester textiles
202. Industrial production of urea (fertilizer)
203. Industrial production of ammonium nitrate fertilizer
204. Physical metallurgy of copper
205. Physical metallurgy of nickel
206. Manufacture of ultraviolet spectroscopes
207. Manufacture of infra-red spectroscopes
208. Manufacturing of guitars
209. Manufacturing of pianos

210. Manufacture of field hockey sticks
211. Manufacture of equipment for ice skating
212. Installing air conditioning in museums
213. Installation of air conditioning in biological museums
214. Installing air conditioning in hospital libraries
215. Installing air conditioners in residential buildings
216. Air conditioning in residential buildings for physically disabled people
217. Depiction of Buddhist themes in art works
218. Medical objects as art works
219. Use of steel in architectural constructions
220. Architecture of buildings for indoor games with special reference to handicapped persons
221. Architecture of multiple purpose auditoriums
222. Architecture of Hindu temples
223. Architecture of library science school buildings
224. Architecture of general library buildings
225. Architecture of hospital libraries
226. Remodelling of hospital libraries
227. Architecture of Bungalows for Solar Energy use
228. Effects of social conditions on the architecture of the National Library of India
229. Architecture of club houses for the aged people
230. Drawing reptiles
231. Drawings of penguins
232. Paintings depicting Indian history
233. Paintings on Indian Moughal history
234. Bird cinematography
235. Photographs of birds
236. Fishing for sharks

237. Sacred music of the Sikhs
238. Sikh sacred music for specific times
239. Orchestra music performances in London
240. A treatise on the recording of violin music.

15

How to Use the Relative Index

The Relative Index (RI) of the DDC22 comprising of 928 pages is contained in the fourth volume. It is an alphabetical key to the DDC schedules, tables, and the manual. Considered as innovative and everlasting contribution of Melvil Dewey to the science of library classification, it is an integral and aboriginal part of the Dewey's system—not merely an adjunct.

It is called relative as all the subjects scattered by discipline in the schedules are brought together in the Relative Index, and the relations between scattered but related concepts (distributed relatives) are displayed in the index. In the schedules the division being by discipline the different aspects of a subject get scattered. In the RI these scattered relatives are brought together and displayed meaningfully showing relations of subordination, coordination, and of related terms. It means that in the index disciplines are subordinated to the subjects. In other words the RI relates a subject to its different disciplines.

The approach here is thus opposite to that of the schedules; and thus is complementary to access the system conceptually. Based on ISO 999 : 1996, *Guidelines for the content, organization and presentation of indexes*, it is an alphabetical list of all the:

a) headings, terms, concepts and notes appended to entries in the schedules (vols. 2-3);

b) terms in the six tables (vol. 1), Introduction and Glossary;

c) and broader concepts in the *Manual* (vol. 1).

Some concepts and terms implied and some terms obtainable through number building but having sufficient literary warrant have also been included in the index. Recognised synonyms of some of the terms (having sufficient literary warrant) have also been included to totally avoid *see* references except the see Manual at ... references. Apart from physiogeographic names and features, countries and their provinces are also included as in Table 2. Other categories of names included are of historical figures like kings, queens, eras, of heads of states, or regimes. Some schools of thought named after persons are there, though individually such persons have not been listed.

Each page of the RI has been divided into two columns by a vertical line in the centre. Each column consists of entries. An entry may be defined as a term or phrase followed by its DDC number on the right. An entry may (or may not) contain subentries, sub-subentries and "*see also*" and "*see Manual* at..." references. For example:

Pisacha literatures	891.499
Pisacha languages	491.499
	T6-91499
Pisces	597
see also Fishes	

All entries are arranged **word by word** with first letter capital of the entry word.

Asia

Asia minor

Asian Americans

Asian flower arrangements

Asians

Asiatic

Subentries shown through indentions begin with a Roman small unless it is a proper name:

Umpiring (Recreation)	790.1
American football	796.332 3
baseball	796.357 3
Canadian football	796.335 3
cricket	796.358 3
rugby	796.333 3
soccer	796.334

Hyphen is treated as a space, i.e., a hyphenated word is treated as two words, e.g.:

Cross River

Cross-stich

Crossbills

or

PI (Macroeconomics)	339.32
Pi-mesons	539.72162
Pi pas	787.82
Piacenza	T2-4546

Different punctuation marks are arranged as follows:

Term

Term. subheading

Term (Parenthetical qualifier)

Term, inverted part qualifier

Term as a phrase

For example

Canada

Canada. Parliament

Canada, Eastern

Canada, Western

Canada goose

Canadian Arctic

Central (Scotland)

Central Africa

or

Pisces	597
Pisces (Zodiac)	133.5277

or

United Nations	341.23
United Nations (Military alliance) World War II	940.5332
United Nations. Charter	341.232
United Nations. General Assembly	341.2322
United Nations. Security Council	341.2323
United Nations Children's Fund	362.7
United Nations treaties Series	341.0262

American spellings have been used throughout

Catalogs	T1-0216
Catalogs (Bibliographic catalogs)	025.31
Labor	331
Labor (Obstetrics)	618.4

Initials and acronym are treated as a word and filed accordingly.

Ablutions

ABM (Missiles)

Aid to families....

AIDS (Disease)

Unemployment insurance

Unesco

Unfair economic practices

Interestingly, initials and acronyms are entered both under the abbreviation and fully spelled form:

Military police (p. 521)	353.13323
MP (Military police (p.541)	353.13323
VCR (Cassette recorders) (p. 881)	384.558
Video cassette recorders (p. 886)	384.558
World Wide Web (p. 918)	0041.678
WWW (p. 918)	044.678

Proper names beginning with numerals are filed before A, i.e., at the beginning of the RI:

100 Mile House (BC)	T2-71175
401 (k) peans	332.0240145
A level examination	378.1662
Aachen (Germany)	T2-435511

Proper names of all sorts are entered according to AACR2R (2002) specifications. Terminology is current and internationally used; American bias is being reduced gradually; commonly used forms of terms have been preferred. Plants and animals have been entered twice both under their taxomonomic and common names. Subjects denoted by a phrase are entered directly. It means that adjectival phrases begin with the adjective:

Agricultural banks

Agricultural credit

Civil engineering

Color television

Islamic calendar

Juda's betrayal of Jesus Christ

Pitman shorthand system

In some cases an adjectival phrase may be broken into a subentry to keep aspects of an important concept together:

India	954
	T2-54
ancient	934
	T2-34

But place names with directions are inverted, however:

Canada, Eastern	T2-713
Canada, Western	T2-712
England, Northern	T2-427

If the direction is a part of the name proper than it is not inverted:

North America	970
North Carolina	975.6
North Korea	951.93

The index is highly structured both semantically and typographically to yield maximum information while conserving space. Use of typographical indentions and syndetic device of "*see also...*" have skilfully been made to depict rank relations and reveal different aspects of the subject indexed. As shown earlier, an entry could be stand alone, i.e., having no subentry or any *see also...* reference:

Dorset (England)	T2-4233
Double cropping	631.58

But many entries have subentries with related concepts beginning with a Roman small and listed alphabetically. For example (p. 652)

Public schools	371.01
elementary	372.10421
finance	379.11
law	344.076
law	344.071
secondary education	373.224
see also Public education	
see also Manual at 371 vs. 353.8, 371.2, 379	
Public schools (United Kingdom)	371.02

The number 371.01 against the (unintended) main entry is the number for general/comprehensive or interdisciplinary works on the subject of public schools. Some major aspects of public schools, namely Elementary public schools, Public schools finance, Law of public schools, and Public schools for secondary education have been listed alphabetically under the main entry "Public schools" leaving one indention to the right alongwith their respective class numbers. The term "law" given as subentry of the subentry finance means "Public schools finance law" has the class number 344.076, whereas the next entry of law means "Law of public schools" has the class number 344.071. Further the index users/classifiers are advised to look under "Public education" for more or related topics on Public schools. *See also* references are to relate broader or synonymous headings for wider choices. "*See also...*" references increase the recall ratio. Further for precise, compared and contrasted interpretation of Public schools the classifiers have been advised to look the *Manual* at some directed places. "*See manual at...*" notes, which are always given in italics, increase the precision ratio.

To repeat, when a topic treated from perspectives of two or more disciplines is represented by multiple numbers, the class number displayed on the index entry opposite the unintended term is the class number for multidisciplinary/

comprehensive or general works on the subject. It is a suggestive number though this multidisciplinary number is repeated under the discipline in which it falls. For example:

Olives	641.3463
agriculture	634.63
botany	583.87
commercial processing	664.80463
cooking	641.6463
food	641.3463

It simply means that all the interdisciplinary works on Olives are placed at 641.3463 though actually it is the number for Olive food. Since the DDC-21 the provision of numbers for interdisciplinary subjects has been enormously increased.

Interdisciplinary numbers do not exist for all subjects for various reasons. In such cases the main entry having subentries is shown blank. For example,

Feudal Age	
European history	940.14
Japanese history	952.02

It simply means that there is no class number for interdisciplinary works on Feudal age.

How to consult the RI:

The index is a list of single and multiworded terms and phrases comprising of names of concepts, entities, persons, places, events, processes, etc., etc, all arranged in a single alphabetical word by word order. A single term is obviously looked into directly. If there is a recognised synonym of the term with sufficient literary warrant then the term is indexed under both; the less preferred term then also refers to the more preferred term with *see also* reference where all other aspects of the subject are indexed as subentries. For example:

Internal commerce	381(p. 409)

see also Domestic trade

It is a less preferred term for Domestic trade (p. 237)

Domestic trade	381
law	343.08
public administration	354.73

Domestic trade is a preferred term as it is a full entry with subentries

Take another example:

Aves 598 (p. 62)

See also Birds

Going to the entry under Birds (p. 86):

Birds	598
agricultural pests	632.68
air transportation hazard	363.12412
animal husbandry	636.5
art representation	704.94328
arts	T3C 3628
commercial hunting	639.12
conservation technology	639.978
control technology	628.968
agriculture	632.68
disease carriers	571.986
medicine	614.434
drawing	743.68
paleozoology	568
resource economics	333.958
sports hunting	799.24
zoology	598

All the varied aspects of birds have been listed alphabetically while two aspects namely control technologies and disease carriers have their subaspects, which may be termed as sub-subaspects of Birds.

For example, Birds as agricultural pests has the class number 632.68. Bird control technology has the class number 628.968. But for 'Bird control technology in/for agriculture, has the class number 632.68.

In a multiworded term having both concrete and abstract words, 'or words denoting an entity or process, we should look first under the concrete term or entity rather than the abstract or process word. For example, for

High seas law

Solar eclipse

Television transmission

Wetlands ecology

Zoology of dogs

We should look under High Seas, Solar, Television, Wetlands and Dogs respectively as these are the concrete entities in the above terms.

Similarly for Ancient India we should look under "India" as it is more concrete than the word ancient. If a term consists of equally concrete or abstract words then such a term may be indexed under both the words. For example "Insurance rates", appears as

Rates (p. 688)

communication industry	384.041
insurance	368.011
transportation services	388.049

and also under Insurance rates 368.011 (p. 406). The term "Insurance rates" has considerable literary warrant.

In the 22nd edition in tune with the LC and Sears subject headings lists and the Library of Congress policies and in accordance with the current thinking in the profession in the days of online and networked information retrieval the adjective phrases are entered directly, i.e., in uninverted form. For example:

Civil engineering	624
Commercial art	741.6
Engineering geology	624.151
Old Spanish language	467.01
Old World rabbits	599.322

In the DDC20 and previous editions these were entered as Engineering, civil; Art, commercial, and so on.

Terms from any of the six tables (in volume 1) or references to the Manual have been indicated so. Full forms of the standard and mnemonic abbreviations for the six tables along with other abbreviations used in the RI are given on page 3, volume 4:

Tl	Table 1	Standard subdivisions
...	....	....
T6	Table 6	Languages

Other abbreviation pertain mostly to the states of the US and other places:

Rabun county (Ga)	Tl-758123
Quorn (S. Aust.)	T2-94236

Here Ga. stands for Georgia state and S. Aust. stands for South Australia. In fact, since the RI of 21st edition, unlike the previous editions, minimum use of abbreviations has been made.

It may be noted that the number from any of the tables are listed next to the interdisciplinary number/or the number of the main entry. It is then followed by subentries (if any) in alphabetical sequence:

Forecasting	003.2
	Tl -0112

business	338.544
investment	332.678
management decision-making	658.40355
marketing management	658.818
occultism	133.3
social change	303.49
weather	551.63

It means that class number for interdisciplinary works on forecasting is 003.2, and the term forecasting also appears in Table 1 Standard subdivisions at 0112. Rest of the aspects of forecasting have been listed alphabetically. Take another example.

India	954
	T2-54
ancient	934
	T2-34

The number for Indian history or interdisciplinary works on India is 954. India also occurs in Table 2 at 54. The number for Ancient India (subentry) is 934 and this term also occurs in Table 2 at 34.

For a reference to any entry or subentry in Manual there is a direct instruction to *see Manual at...* a particular reference:

Miniatures	688.1
	T1-0228
handicrafts	745.5928
see Manual at 745.5928	
manufacturing technology	688.1

The instruction *see Manual at..* always appears in italics. It is clear from the indention that *see Manual at* 745.5928 is a subentry of handicrafts and not of the main entry Miniatures. It means that for discussion/explanation of classification of miniature handicrafts the classifier should consult the manual at number 745.5928 (p 150, vol. 1). There is a long note for different possible numbers for handicrafted miniatures and models. The manual provides relevant and free discussion about the topic for comparison and contrast with other related or seemingly similar topics and their class numbers. The manual provides information for better interpretation of an entry. However in the DDC22 references to the manual have been reduced.

No index can be totally exhaustive, so is the Relative Index; index is not an alphabetical recapitulation of the schedules and tables. The categories of terms not included have been listed at Section 11.15 of the Introduction (p. lxii, vol. 1). These are "phrases beginning with the adjective form of countries, languages, nationalities, religious, e.g., English poetry, French cooking, Italian architecture, Hindu prayer books". Exceptions are the cases with a strong literary warrant, e.g., English literature. If the name is a unique proper noun then it may be included, e.g., English channel, Indian ocean, Indian hemp., French bulldog. Other category of excluded terms is the concepts divisible by standard subdivisions, e.g., Science dictionaries, Research in religions.

If a concept is not found directly then its broader class may be looked for to arrive at some base number. For example, for a class number on Jawaharlal Nehru University we should look under universities; for a biography of Kapil Dev we should look under cricket, where the appropriate term seems cricket players. As an another example, for Bahadur Shah Zafar, the last Mughal King, we should look under "Mughal Empire". As another example, for postal rates we should look under "Ratest–communications industry".

The Relative index if properly operated brings alive many topics buried in the schedules. This is in line with the index of the previous edition, DDC-21. It is simple and smart, and easy to use.

16

Answers to Exercises for Self Practice

(A) Use of standard subdivisions

1. 382.9209
2. 153.940005
3. 351.072041
4. 381.12+065 (as under 380) + 43 (T_2; as under 065) = 381.1206543
5. 512.0072
6. 512.0072054
7. 025.4900072041
8. 684.10029+54(T2)=684.1002954
9. 070.0711+1724(T2)=070.07111724
10. 070.09034
11. 072.09034
12. 079.17124109034
13. 079.1767
14. 079.176709034

15. 079+54 (Table 2) + 09175 (Table 1) + 69 (Table 6) = 079.540917569
16. 071.109034
17. 070+082(Table 1)=070.082
18. 070.4082
19. 070+089(Table l)+914122(Table 5)=070.089914122
20. 330.9+54+009(Table l)+176(from Table 2)+7 (from 297 of schedules) = 330.9540091767
21. 330.9+54(T2)+009(ss Tl)+l 761 (T2)=330.9540091761
22. 330.9+54(T2)+04(from 954.04)=330.95404
23. 320.960091716
24. 303.4+09(T1)+175(T2)+9143(T6)+0+54(T2)= 303.4091759143054 (see option under -1 Areas in general (T2) p. 217, vol. 1)
25. 307.14+1(as under 307.1-307.3) +2(from 307.72) + 09(T1) + 54 (T2) = 307.14120954
26. 909.09+724(from Table 2, from 1724)=909.09724
27. 909.09724+0+826(from909.826)=909.097240826
28. 909.09717
29. 909.09+761(from 1761(T2))+0+8(from 909.8)=909.0976108
30. 909.09+75(from l75(T2))+21(T6)=909.097521

(B) Titles requiring addition of two areas from Table 2

31. 304.8+73+0+54=304.873054

    Note that the country towards which migration occurs is to be taken first and the place of origin comes as latter facet.
32. 304.8+73+0+1724=304.87301724
33. 304.8+4(T2)+0+176(T2)+43(from 294.3)=304.8401 7643
34. 332.456091+73+0+54=332.45609173054
35. 332.4560914041

36. 325.3+41+09+5=325.341095
37. 325.3+41+09+1824=325.341091824
38. 709.5409+176(Table2)+7(from 297 of schedules)
= 709.54091767
39. 704.08+8(from 088(T1)+297 (schedules) = 704.088297
40. 704.03+96073(T5)=704.0396073
41. 332.673+41+0+1724=332.6734101724
42. 332.6737305491
43. 325.2+54+0+73=325.254073
44. 327+51+0+73=327.51073
45. 327.7301717
46. 327+5694(T2)+0+176(T2)+7(from 297 schedules)
= 327.569401767
47. 327+5694(T2)+0+176(T2)+7(from297)+0+5(T2)
= 327.56940176705
(Third area facet has been added as per option under -1(T2) p. 217, vol. 1)
48. 327+54(Table 2)+0+1712(Table 2)+41(Table 2) =327.540171241
49. 327.0917124105
50. 331.62+5496+0+54=331.625496054
51. 331.62+5491 +0+56=331.625491056
52. 338.91+54+0+5496=338.915405496
53. 338.917301724
54. 338.911+712 (from 1712 (T2)+41(T2)+0+1724(T2)
= 338.9117124101724
55. 338.91+47(T2)+0+1717(T2)+0+4(T2)=338.91470171704
56. 382.09+52+0+71=382.0952071
57. 382.09171701724

58. 382.9+54(T2)+0+73(T2)=382.954073
59. 382.911+716(from l716(T2))=382.911716
60. 027.4091724
61. 379.129+5496(T2)+0+54(T2)=379.1295496054

(C) Illustrations Depicting Synthesis in the Schedules

62. 025.19+77(from 027.7)=025.1977
63. 025.19+77(from 027.7)+54(T2)as under 027.7)=025.197754
64. 025.218+77(from 027.7)=025.21877
65. 025.218+7665(from 027.665)=025.2187665
66. 025.27+341=025.27341
67. 025.27+9737=025.279737
68. 025.27+0252=025.270252
69. 025.28+34(from 025.3434)=025.2834
70. 025.28+94(from025.3494)=025.2894
71. 025.27+5=025.275 (This is the officially preferred number)

    or

    025.28+32(from025.3432)=025.2832
72. 025.527+7625(from 027.625)=025.5277625
73. 070.449+500=070.4495
74. 070.449+796=070.449796
75. 153.94+610=153.9461
76. 153.94+070=153.9407
77. 155.45+12(digits following 371.9: The number for deaf children being 371.912)=155.4512
78. 156.2+4(from 152.1-152.8)=156.24
79. 220.8+52=220.852
80. 221+5(from 220.1-220.8)+9143 (Table 6) =221.59143

81. 222+0 (as instructed under 221-229)+5(from 220.5) +9143(T6) =222.059143
82. 222.16+0+5+9143=222.16059143
83. 225+5(from 220.1-220.8)+9143(Table 6) =225.59143
84. 230(as instructed under 230.1 -.9)+15(from 281-289 where Eastern churches are 281.5)

    230.15
85. 294.4+35(from 203.5 as under 290 p. 261, vol.2)=294.435
86. 294.4+36=294.436
87. 331.1241+025(from schcdules)=331.1241025
88. 331.124+30(from 630)=331.1243

    (We have added to the base 331.124, the digits following 6 in 620-690. The class number for agriculture is 630.)
89. 331.1291+020=331.129102
90. 331.129+30(from 630)=331.1293
91. 331.204+30=331.2043
92. 331.281+025=331.281025
93. 331.28+30=331.283
94. 331.8811+020=331.881102
95. 331.881+30=331.8813
96. 331.89041+025=331.89041025
97. 331.8904+30=331.89043
98. 331.89281+025=331.89281025
99. 331.8928+30=331.89283 .
100. 334.681+025=334.681025
101. 334.68+30=334.683
102. 338.17+65 (from 633-638, where poultry is 636.5) =338.1765
103. 338.27+4(from553.2-553.9)=338.274
104. 328.549602

105. 362.19+6994 (from 616-618)=362.196994
106. 362.19+6994+24(from 611.2-611.9)
= 362.19699424
107. 362.19+6998 (from 616.998) =362.196998
108. 362.292+5 (from special sub-divisions under 362-363) +24 (from 361.2-361.8)=362.292524
109. 362.293 + 86(as under 362-363) = 362.29386
110. 362.3+85(as under 362-363)=362.385
111. 363.3493+83(as under 362-363)=363.349383
112. 371.926+3(from 371 .9043-371 .9047)=371 .9263
113. 371 .9280+5(from 371 .9043)=371 .92805
114. 372.1+542(from 371.542) =372.1542
115. 372.1+335(from 371.335)=372.1335
116. 372.35+043 (Special sub-divisions under 372.3-372.8, vol. 2 : 800) =372.35043
117. 373.1 +542 (from 371.1-371.8) =373.1542
118. 373.1 +335 =373.1335
119. 378.17+35 (from 371 .3028-371 .397 where AVs are 371.335) =378. 1735
120. 372.1(from 372.11-.18)+716 (from 371.716) = 372.1716
121. 398.2452+967 (from 592-599, where the elephant is 599.67) =398.2452967
122. 398.2492+967(from 597.67 elephants)+l(as under 592-599)+513(from 591.513 Animal intelligence) = 398.24929671513
123. 398.368+3734 (from 582-588 where rose is 583.734) = 398.3683734
124. 523.98+6 (from 523.43-523.48 where Saturn is 523.46) = 523.986
125. 523.98+6+3(from 523.33 orbit)=523.9863
126. 529.32+45 (from 292-299 where the Hindu religion is 294.5)=529.3245

127. 539.737+62 (from 539.7211-539.7217 where mesons are 539.72162) =539.73762
128. 546.396+5 (special subdivision under 546 vol. 2, p. 1021) +88 (from 541. 33-54 1.39)=546.396588
129. 547.1+3 (from 541.2-541.7) =547.13
130. 547.1+3884 (from 541.2-547.7)=547.13884
131. 547.01+045 (special subdivisions under 547)+884 (from 541.33-547.39) =547.01045884
132. 547.61+045+884 (from 541.33-541.39) =547.61045884
133. 572.36+2(from 571.2)=572.362
134. 572+2(from 571.2)+6(from 586 cryptogamia)=572.26
135. 571.4+2(from 571 .2)+6(from 586)=571.426
136. 572.36+2(from 571.2)+6(from 586)=572.3626
137. 572+l(from571.1)=572.1
138. 572.36+l(from 571.1)=572.361
139. 572.565+l(from 571.1 as given under 572.5-572.8) =572.5651
140. 572.6+l(from 571.1)=572.61
141. 572.579+1 (from 571.1)+2(from 592)=572.57912
142. 572.565+l(from 571.1)+57(from 595.7)=572.565157
143. 572+l(from 571.1)+5726(from 595.726)=572. 15726
144. 572.36+l(from 571.1)+5726(from 595.726)=572.3615726
145. 572.7+l(from 571. l)+5726(from 595.726)=572.715726
146. 612.9+1 (from 611.91-611.98 where the head is 6I1.91)=612.91
147. 615.31+5 (from 547.01-547.08 where organometallic compounds is 547.05)=615.315
148. 615.31+61 (from 547.01-547.08 where sulfite compounds is 547.061)=615.3161
149. 615.31+5+673 (Following 546 in 546.38-546.72, where aluminium is 546.673)=615.315673

150. 615.31+5+383 (from 546.38-546.72 where potassium is 546.383)=615.315383

151. 615.925+652 (from 546.2-546.7 where copper is 546.652)=615.925652

152. 615.925+688=615.925688

153. 616.24+07 (as instructed under 616.1-616.9 where pathology is 07)+5(from 616.071-616.079 where diagnosis is 616.075)=616.24075

154. 616.24+07+547(from616.07547)=616.2407547

155. 616.912 Smallpox is an asterisked class; at the footnote we have been asked to add special subject divisions as instructed under 616.1-616.9(v3:85-86)there therapies is 06; and to specify various therapies, we have been asked to add to 06 the digits following 615.8 in 615.82-615.89, and spurious therapies is 615.856. Hence,

616.912+06+56=616.9120656

156. 616.71 +06+45(from615.845)=616.710645

157. 616.722+06+45=616.7220645

158. 616.995+06+34(from615.834)=616.9950634

159. Tuberculosis is 616.995; for tuberculosis of a specific organ, we have been asked to divide 616.995 like 611.1-611.9, where bone is 611.71, hence the class number for bone TB is 616.995+71=616.99571

The special subject subdivisions given under 616.1-616.8 are still applicable here. Hence: 616.99571+06+34=616.995710634 is the required number.

160. 616.995+71 (from 611.1-611.9)+07(special subdivisions under 616.1-616.9)+572(from 616.071-616.079) =616.9957107572

161. 617.15+2(from 611.711-611.718 where ribs is 611.712)=617.152

162. 617.63+061 (from special divisions under 617)=617.63061

163. 617.632+06+45 (from 615.82-615.89 where electrotherapy is 615.845)=617.6320645

164. 618.920 (from 618.92001-618.92009) + 09 (from special sub divisions under 616.1-616.9, where case histories is 09)=618.92009

165. 621.322+76 (from 725-728 where museum buildings is 727.6)=621.32276

166. 621.322+76+5(from 011-999) = 621.322765

167. 621.322+76+570 (from 001-999 where biology is 570)=621.3227657

168. 621.322+5822+(Theater is 725.822)=621. 3225822

169. 621.322+782 (from 725-728 where general libraries is 727.82)+662 (from 027.1-027.8 where hospital libraries is 027.662)=621.322782662

170. 624.153+36(from 620.12-620.19 where concrete is 620.136)=624.15336

171. 629.287+72 (from 629.2204-629.229, where bicycles is 629.2272)=629.28772

172. 630.2 (from 630.21-29) +40 (from 510-590)=630.24

173. 630.2+413 (from 510-590 where physical chemistry is 541.3)=630.2413

174. 634.04+89 (from special subdivisions under 633-635 as per instruction on page v3:310)=634.0489

175. 634.04+89+42 (from 631.81-631.89) where nitrate fertilizer is 631.842)=634.048942

176. 634.304+89+42=634.3048942

177. 635.91+842 (from 631.2-631.8)=635.91842

178. 636.50+855 (from 636.001-636.08 where feed is 636.0855) = 636.50855

179. 639.39+6 (from 597.92-597.98 where snakes is 597.96)= 639.396

180. 638.57+89 (from 595.789) + 0 + 5(T2) = 638.578905

181. 639.396+09548=639.39609548

182. 641.3(from 641.33-.35)+31 (from 633-635 where cereals is 633.1)=641.331

183. 646.453+0+4(from 646.404)=646.45304

184. 649.15+3 (from 371.91-371.95; 371.93)=649.153

185. 649.15+12(from 371.912)=649.1512

186. 649.157+924 (from Table 5 for Jews)=649.157924

187. 649.157924+0+73=649.157924073

188. 649.157+9142+0+71=649.1579142071

189. 657.8322+0+42 (from 657.1-657.7 where cost accounting is 657.42)=657.8322042

190. 657.835+0+42=657.835042

191. 657.8322+0+452=657.83220452

192. 661.0+711(from 546.4-546.7 where nitrogen is 546.711) =661.0711

193. 660.29+6(from 541.33-541.39 where thermochemistry is 541.36) =660.296

194. 662.622+5(from 553.21-553.25 where anthracite coal is 553.25) =662.6225

195. 663.20+5(from 663.11-663.19 where pasteurization is 663.15) =663.205

196. 666.3+5(from ss 01-09)=666.35

It is a rare exception where a standard subdivision has been added without its featured zero.

197. 666.3+72(from ss 072)=666.372

198. 666.3+72+0+73(area)=666.372073

199. 666.3+6+0+54=666.36054

200. 667.3+39(from 677.1-677.5 where silk is 677.39)=667.339

201. 667.3+4743=667.34743

202. 668.62+41 (from 631.83-631.85 where urea is 631.841) =668.6241

203. 668.62+42=668.6242
204. 669.96+3(from 669.1-669.7 where copper is 669.3)= 669.963
205. 669.96+7332=669.967332
206. 681.414+4 (from 535.842-535.846 where ultraviolet light *is* 535.844)=681.4144
207. 681.414+2=681.4142
208. 681.8+787 (from 786-788 where the guitar is 787.87) =681.8787
209. 681.8+62=681.862
210. 688.76+355(from 796.1-796.9 where field hockey is 796.355)=688.76355
211. 688.76+91 (from 796.91)=688.7691
212. 697.93+76 (from 725-728 where museum buildings is 727.6) =697.9376
213. 697.93+76+570 (from 001-999 where biology is 570) =697.937657
214. 697.93+782(from 725-728 where general libraries is 727.82)+662 (from 027.1-027.8 where hospital libraries is 027.662)=697.93782662
215. 697.93+8=697.938
216. 697.93+8 (from 728)+087(as under 721-729)=697.938087
217. 704.9489+43 (following 29 in 292-299, where Buddhism is 294.3) =704.948943
218. 704.949+61 (from 000-999)=704.94961
219. 721.0447+142(from 669.1-669.7, where steel is 669.142)=721.0447142
220. 725.84+087(from T_1 Std sub)=725.84087
221. 725.83+04(as under 721-729)+9(from 720.49)=725.83049
222. 726.1+45(from 292-299 where Hinduism is 294.5) =726.145

223. 727.4+02(from 001-999)=727.402

Whereas the architecture of library buildings is placed at 727.8 which is amenable to further expansion.

224. 727.82

225. 727.82+662(from 027.662)=727.82662

226. 727.82+662+0286(v3:559)=727.826620286

227. 728.373 + 04 + 72 (from 720.472) = 728.3730472

228. 727.82+5(from 027.5)+54(Area Table)+010(at 721-729) +3(from 700.103)=727.825540103

229. 728.4+0846 (T_1-Std sub)=728.40846

230. 743.6+79 (from 592-599, where reptiles is 597.9)=743.679

231. 743.6+847 (from 592-599 where penguins is 598.47)=743.6847

232. 758.9+954(from 001-999)=758.9954

233. 758.9+954025=758.9954025

234. 778.538+598(from 001-999)=778.538598

235. 779+32(from 704.9432)+8(from 598)=779.328

236. 799.17+3 (from 597.2-597.5, where sharks is 597.3) =799.173

237. 781.7+46 (from 294-299 where Sikhism is 294.6) =781.746

238. 781.7+46 (from 294.6)+0(as under 784.74-. 79)+523(from 781.523)=781.7460523

239. 784.2+078 (from 784-744 and 780.78) + 421 (T2) = 784.2078421

240. 787.20266 (from 780.266)

Index